Chasing Grace

Chasing Grace

*Reflections of a
Catholic Girl,
Grown Up*

Martha Manning

HarperSanFrancisco
An Imprint of HarperCollins*Publishers*

CHASING GRACE: *reflections of a Catholic girl, grown up.* Copyright © 1996 by Martha Manning. All rights reserved. Printed in the United States of America. No part of this book may be used or reproduced in any manner whatsoever without written permission except in the case of brief quotations embodied in critical articles and reviews. For information address Harper-Collins Publishers, 10 East 53rd Street, New York, NY 10022.

HarperCollins Web Site: http://www.harpercollins.com

HarperCollins®, ♦®, and HarperSanFrancisco™ are trademarks of HarperCollins Publishers Inc.

FIRST EDITION

Library of Congress Cataloging-in-Publication Data
Manning, Martha.
    Chasing grace : reflections of a Catholic girl, grown up / Martha Manning.—1st ed.
    ISBN 0–06–251311–7 (cloth)
    ISBN 0–06–251312–5 (pbk.)
    1. Manning, Martha. 2. Biography—memoir. 3. Psychotherapists—United States—Biography. I. Title.
BX4705.M3115A3   1996
282'.092—dc20   96–6773

96 97 98 99 00 ❖ RRD (H) 10 9 8 7 6 5 4 3 2 1

for my parents
John and Mary Louise Manning
with infinite gratitude and love

Being Irish, he had an
abiding sense of tragedy
which sustained him through
temporary periods of joy.

—*W. B. Yeats*

Contents

Contents

Preface

FROM THE FIRST GRADE I knew the words by heart: "A sacrament is an outward sign instituted by Christ, to give grace." I could tick off the list of sacraments in synchrony with my classmates: baptism, penance, Eucharist, confirmation, holy orders, marriage, and last rites. The concept of grace, however, was a tough one to actually wrap my hands around. Grace is defined as "unmerited divine assistance given man for his regeneration or sanctification." As a seven-year-old, I knew basically that grace was a good thing, that I wanted to pile up as much of it as I could, and that sin would deplete my resources.

Years later, I don't have much to add to that assessment. We strive to be in a "state of grace," to avoid a "fall from grace," to be "graced," "graceful," and "gracious." Yet most of us struggle with the inadequacy of language as we reach for the description of what grace actually is. I've always loved the reply of Saint Joan of Arc when her ecclesiastical judges attempted to set her up for a fall.

Asked if she was in a state of God's grace, she answered: "If I am not, may it please God to put me in it; if I am, may it please God to keep me there."

While there are infinite ways to gain grace, the sacraments are offered as both concrete and symbolic rituals that confer grace. They mark a moment in a person's spiritual life in which she moves from one stage to the next. But a sacrament is so much more than a ritual. It takes longer than a moment. It is a lifetime process—never something that is actually achieved. We walk toward it our entire lives, circling round and round it, sometimes hitting close to the target, sometimes missing entirely.

Sacraments define the essence of the gifts and challenges of any life. Their meaning transcends membership in a certain sect or denomination and serves instead as a series of markers in a person's journey from birth to death. The themes of the sacraments are the continual answers to the continual question, What exactly is it that we're all supposed to be doing here?

While the sacraments I describe are rooted in Catholic theology, their true meaning cannot be limited by specific doctrines or dogmas. In fact, *most* religions emphasize and observe particular and critical points in a person's life, telling us how to search for that elusive state of grace, for a connectedness with the sacred, even when it is totally beyond our comprehension or control.

The purpose of this book is to tell the story of these themes as they resonate over the years of my own life—from my early years in the constricted security of a typical Catholic childhood, to the present in which my religious status is diffuse, leaving me on good days feeling like a pilgrim and on bad days like I'm homeless.

Sacraments center on the most basic human needs and struggles: loving, belonging, receiving, hurting, forgiving, needing, claiming, believing, committing, sacrificing, suffering, and letting go. I wrestle daily with these themes, sometimes successfully, sometimes unsuccessfully. Most of the time I'm somewhere in between, with great intentions and clumsy follow-through.

SOME YEARS AGO, my mother-in-law and three Catholic nuns drove into downtown Washington, D.C., for a performance of the

National Symphony. Before the trip, the nuns attested to their absolute confidence about the directions. As they got closer to their destination, however, each turn the nuns instructed my mother-in-law to take was the result of an impromptu vote, which was never unanimous.

After thirty minutes, my mother-in-law realized that they were driving in circles, in an area where the danger increases dramatically with the darkness. It appeared that only my mother-in-law was aware that they were lost in the highest-crime-rate neighborhood in a city that always competes for the honor of murder capital of the country. She was astounded that the nuns appeared not the slightest bit concerned about their predicament. They chatted along and every now and then had a brainstorm about suddenly remembering the directions.

After reaching her tolerance of frustration and fear, my mother-in-law exploded: "WHAT IS THE MATTER WITH YOU? WE ARE TERRIBLY, HORRIBLY LOST IN THE ABSOLUTE WORST PART OF THE CITY! DON'T YOU REALIZE THAT WE COULD BE KILLED?" The nuns responded with the kind of benign, but bewildered look one would give a person who ran screaming from a room at the sight of a tiny insect. Sister Jane Ann, my mother-in-law's best friend since childhood, reached across the seat and patted my mother-in-law on the arm, saying gently but with great conviction, "Oh, Jane, don't worry. We're all in a state of grace."

My mother-in-law was dumbfounded by the absolute naïveté of this response. By the next morning, she had conveyed it to us all, numerous times, communicating her incredulity that those grown, otherwise competent women could have seen themselves as so completely protected in such treacherous surroundings.

Her story always gets laughs from those of us who live in the "real world." Whenever she recounts it, her ending is always the same.

"Can you *believe* that?"

I'VE LOVED THAT STORY for as long as she's told it, enjoying yet another example of the ridiculous faith of the "religious." But lately I think of those nuns, lost in a dark city, with the firmest of faith despite the flimsiest of directions, and I wonder how one actually gets to that "state of grace." And now, when my mother-in-law laughingly asks the rhetorical, "Can you *believe* that?" I want to answer, in all seriousness, "No, but I'd really like to."

❧ THE CHOSEN ONE

I BEGAN EAVESDROPPING early in life, fascinated by the information adults reserve only for one another. Throughout my childhood I always felt I lacked that one significant piece of information that would help me make sense of the many things I didn't understand. So I remedied my ignorance as best I could, either by asking for information directly—which always yielded incomplete and useless responses—or by stealing it. Mine was a good neighborhood for eavesdropping. In the late afternoons, four or five mothers gathered around a backyard picnic table, downing cocktails, relating the trials of the day, and talking about their "real" lives—the lives that were somehow separate from us, their children.

It was the only time we got to see them in anything other than their roles as "Mom." Even though we would inevitably interrupt them in midsentence, forcing at least one mother to glare in the direction of trouble and scream, "Jimmy, I told you, no rocks in your mouth!" or "I don't *care* who started it. Work it out or we're going home!" their conversations slipped effortlessly from one subject to another. They were old friends, women united by the location of their houses, the colleges they had attended, their husbands' occupations, or the sheer numbers of children in their care. I always wondered what mothers talked about with such animation. What doubled them over with so much laughter that it could carry my mother into a great mood for the rest of the evening? What was happening when the mothers leaned across the picnic table and focused on the tears of another, their arms around her shoulders, their hands over hers? What made mothers cry?

The best place to eavesdrop was in my own house, hidden by a wall thick enough to conceal me but thin enough to carry sound. It was better than television.

The best time for eavesdropping was at the many parties and spontaneous get-togethers my parents had with their close circle of friends. There was always a nucleus that outlasted everyone else, staying up all night, drinking, smoking, and talking. My mother and three or four other women were regulars. Fortunately for me, alcohol had a certain disinhibiting effect on the content of the conversations, as well as the volume.

We older kids in the neighborhood loved those nights because if we got up early enough the next morning, we could accompany our mothers to 6:00 A.M. Sunday mass. They would still be in their party clothes, smelling of alcohol, smoke, and perfume, sometimes even a little silly, which always made the service much more interesting. Our mothers, usually the paragons of upright worship, often struggled in those early mornings to suppress giggles that I thought only children had to manage. These were the only times our mothers ever agreed to stop for doughnuts on the way home. Then, as they registered the sight of the rest of their waking children, and the prospect of a new day on no sleep, our mothers drowned themselves in coffee and regret. And we prepared to stay out of their way.

It was in these late-night conversations that I began to learn what it was really like to be a grown-up. By the time I was twelve, I knew that Mr. Hardy's cheerful exterior was due, almost entirely, to alcohol. I learned which husbands kept their wives on tight leashes, always demanding more than they gave. I discovered that even grown-ups felt and said bad things about their parents— often the same things kids said: they weren't fair, they didn't listen, they were overly critical and demanding. I heard about Mr. McNulty's reasons for leaving home and the "whisperings" of divorce, which made me reevaluate my notion of marriage as an absolutely immutable state with no variation. I thought you were either married or you weren't. Happiness had nothing to do with it. Over the years in those conversations, I learned about the many gradations of the grown-up brand of happy. I learned who was happy, who wasn't, and why. Eavesdropping on those people in the night made them forever different to me in the day.

One night, as the conversation loosened by the hour, I heard the hard-core night owls discussing their children. My ears really perked up, because even though I believed that mothers were put on this earth for the sole purpose of caring for children, I never heard them talk about us very much in their free time. As the only one with a bedroom on the first floor, I was situated perfectly to crack my door, lie in the dark, and hear every single word they said.

My mother and her friends started talking about potential problems with the people their children might marry. Of course, the first and most likely hurdle was a child marrying a "non-Catholic," which, for all intents and purposes, meant Protestant. They all felt that they could handle it, although some worried about the reactions of their parents. Then they progressed to the possibility of their children meeting, dating, and marrying Jews, a fairly high likelihood where we lived on Long Island. There was a definite split on this issue, with the majority agreeing that dating Jewish boys and girls would be fine, but marriage would be too complicated, especially when it came to the question of "the children." Then for some reason, they started talking about who would most likely marry a black person and why. Mrs. Burns bet that her oldest daughter would do it out of spite and that the marriage would never last. My mother volunteered that I would be the most likely of her daughters to marry a black man and that my marriage would last. I found this whole line of discussion puzzling since, to my knowledge, I had never met a black man, and I wasn't aware that my mother had either.

It was beginning to sound like a low-yield evening and I rolled over to call it a night. The clarity of their distinct voices merged into one low and distant hum that faded as I gave myself to sleep. But then I heard a word—a really important word—that yanked me back to the conversation. Someone said the word *favorite*. I rolled over and strained to hear the context, fully planning to return to sleep if they were talking about plays, restaurants, or brands of paint. But they weren't talking about places or things; they were talking about kids. *Their* kids.

They were talking about their favorite kids. It was the biggest bombshell in my career as an eavesdropper. I had never been ambivalent about eavesdropping before. Somehow, all the information I'd gleaned in the past had proved useful, at some point, in understanding the world. But this was different. The knowledge stolen from this conversation could be harmful. I so much wanted to listen but was terrified of what I might hear. All of a sudden, I realized that it is possible to know too much. Just the revelation that mothers even thought about who they loved most was mind-boggling.

Even though I constantly balked and bitched about the inequities in our household, I never questioned my mother's insistence that she loved us (even when she didn't particularly like us) all the same. Had it been just another mother line like "I don't care what everybody else does, you are not . . ." or "As long as you live under this roof . . ."? *Did* mothers have deep-down favorites? I knew there could be tremendous variability in a big family about who was the least annoying kid or the most helpful, sick, or needy on any given day, and maybe for that day those particular kids got to sit under a mother's sun longer than her other kids. I just figured it all evened out in the end. But an *all-time* favorite? The concept was almost too much to bear. Unless, of course, it was I, and then it would be all right. But not really. Because a favorite can fall so easily from grace and become an "unfavorite." The risk wasn't worth it. Equal was probably best.

Mrs. Crosby spoke first. She named her favorite child. Her choice surprised me. I would have put money on her youngest.

With each turn, I was more interested, appalled, and anxious. Mrs. Burns revealed her favorite. No big surprise. Mrs. Finnerty not only shared her favorite, she upped the ante by naming her least favorite. Now I was in double jeopardy, not only of being passed over as *best*, but also of possibly being designated as *worst*.

My mother was the only one left. There was silence, and I could tell that she wasn't exactly jumping into the conversation. My mouth went dry. I could feel my heart kicking against my chest. I didn't know whether to stick my head out and listen or slam my pillow over my head and crawl down under the covers as far as I could go. It was something that I was dying to know—but it could kill me in the knowing.

Mrs. Finnerty pushed my mother, "Come on, Mary Lou. Your turn." My mother protested loudly, "I don't have a favorite." No one believed her and they said so vociferously. I was perched on the edge of my pillow and covers, ready to take a dive if she got any closer to the truth. They kept prodding and she kept insisting, "I love all my children the same. Really . . . I love them all the same."

My memory stops right there. To this day I don't know whether I immediately fell into the relieved sleep of knowing that I was fairly loved, or whether I listened longer to the conversation and, as my mother's resolve crumbled, actually heard her name her favorite. With 95 percent of myself, I think that the first is true.

But 5 percent of me is still the cynical psychologist who believes we block out what is just too damn painful to bear.

✤ TROUBLE

LIFE WAS FAIR during my brief eleven-month reign as an only child. Then my brother came along—the brother who followed me everywhere, stole my toys, and claimed my mother's lap as his own. Over the next thirteen years, with the next four siblings, I became increasingly vigilant about the issues of favorites and fairness.

In my family, each kid picked on the next one down, carrying on the rich tradition of cruelty that I, as the oldest, initiated. One standard torture that stood the test of time was the children's version of Kafka's *Trial*. It happened whenever my mother assigned one kid the job of running up and down the street to collect everyone else for dinner. The gatherer would run up to a younger sibling and sputter breathlessly, "You've gotta go home *right now!* Mom wants you. You are in *soooo* much trouble!" The kid, looking panicked, would search his or her inventory of badness for that day and ask anxiously, "Why?" To which the gatherer would only shrug and reply, "I don't know, but Mom is *really* mad!"

The stooge would then tear down the street, run sweating and tremulous into the house, and present him- or herself to my mother, ready to beg for mercy. My mother would then look up casually from what she was doing, register the appearance of another kid, and say something like "Oh, good. Go wash your hands." The kid would wait, just to make sure our mother wasn't confusing him or her with someone else. About that time the instigator would enter the kitchen, sporting a superior smile, and it would slowly dawn on the kid that he or she had been duped.

You'd think the scam would have stopped right there, but it didn't. We just kept embellishing it each time. The next time, when the stooge expressed distrust, we'd say earnestly, "Oh yeah, I know I was fooling *last* time . . . but *this* time, really . . . you *are* in big trouble. Mom even called Dad at work!" or "You really better run home . . . Mom's even crying!" And so on, to the point where we'd report that our mother was dialing the police as we were leaving.

The middle children got it the worst. With ten and thirteen years between me and my youngest brother and sister, I felt much more like a nurturing mother than a jealous sibling. But Sarah and Priscilla were fair game.

In addition to the you-are-in-so-much-trouble scam, my brother Chip and I developed another, which also had a long life owing to our creative alterations as Sarah and Priscilla began to question our veracity. So that we could get them to finish our chores, we always promised them "a big surprise." They'd dive in, perform the tasks, and then run to us for their surprise, at which point we would give them a big kiss on the cheek. Not exactly what they expected.

When they protested to us, we feigned innocence, swearing that we had never actually lied. When they whined to my mother, she warned us not to "take advantage," which was ridiculous, since that was precisely the point. The next time we tried it, we'd swear to God that it wouldn't be a kiss. They'd do the job, and then we'd reward them with a hearty handshake. It made them crazy.

The stakes grew over time, but never to where there was an even exchange of goods for services. We promised them money and then gave them a penny. We promised to let them play with one of our toys and then picked the worst one and let them use it for only thirty seconds. I originally attributed their limitless capacity to be hoodwinked to stupidity. But on another level I knew it was because they wanted so much to believe in us, to have our favor, to be our friends. I dismissed my own cruelty as just a series of ingenious but innocent pranks. On a deeper level, however, they were acts of war, and I knew it. They were the way my brother and I continued to reinforce our crumbling seniority, which had lost most of its perks but had continually gained in its burdens.

Other scams focused on a particular child. For years we told the fourth child, Priscilla, that she was adopted. We stressed that it was a big secret and warned that if she ever asked my parents, they would deny it. We explained that because my father was a Chinese espionage expert in the FBI, he spent a lot of time in New

York's Chinatown, often interviewing people in Chinese restaurants and laundries. We told Priscilla, whose eyes slanted up ever so slightly, that my father had found her in a basket of shirts at a Chinese laundry and brought her home to live with us.

She ran in tears to my mother, who told her that of course she wasn't adopted.

When she came back to us satisfied of her true heritage, we reminded her that parents *never* admit to children that they were adopted. When she protested, we pointed out that she didn't look like anyone else in the family, which was true. We challenged her to find her baby pictures, of which there were very few. She didn't yet know that for the fourth child in six years, picture taking was a luxury—she was lucky to be fed regularly.

My mother told us to cut it out. She produced one or two baby pictures to reassure Priscilla and shut us all up. But in bed that night, in the room Sarah and I shared with her before we moved and I got my own room, we'd whisper that those were not really pictures of her, but of one of our cousins.

Unlike the rest of us, Priscilla didn't even have a letter from J. Edgar Hoover congratulating my parents on her birth. We pointed this out to her as the ultimate proof. The truth was that she *did* have a letter, but when the director was originally informed of my sister's birth, my parents had chosen the name Victoria. By the time she left the hospital, my parents changed their minds and named her Priscilla. We explained the J. Edgar Hoover letter by saying that my parents had been ready to adopt a child named Victoria, but then, when my father stumbled over Priscilla in the Chinese laundry basket, they took her instead. No one believes that story today, and yet, at least once a year (when our own children aren't listening), we still tease Priscilla mercilessly, and she still protests.

Middle children have two choices in responding to these torments: capitulate or toughen up. The you-are-in-so-much-trouble scam backfired on us years later. Priscilla absolutely hated high school. So she didn't go very much. She made up an amazing range of excuses for her many absences. We all knew that her attendance record was far from stellar, but we had no idea that by her sophomore year she had already far surpassed the three oldest of us in the combined amount of skipping that we had done in our entire high-school tenures.

From the excuse notes Priscilla wrote, the Sisters of the Sacred Heart must have thought our family descended directly from Job. My father wasn't living at home (true, but it was because he was assigned to the "goon squad," a year in which agents conducted surprise office inspections of other FBI offices). Priscilla gave most of us serious illnesses or moral lapses. A couple of us were dangerously close to death or jail. Through these bogus notes, Priscilla accumulated at least fifty missed school days, and the academic year wasn't nearly over. The shit hit the fan when a nun called home and inquired about my mother's failing health.

A brief interchange over the phone illuminated the gravity of Priscilla's offenses. Chip and I had stopped by the house to do our laundry and freeload a meal. Sarah filled us in quickly as we walked in the door. Despite the fact that we were always at one another's throats and never minded seeing someone get in a little trouble, we had sympathy for the *big* stuff. As the three oldest, we had all gotten caught on big stuff before. We knew from cumulative experience that, once you were nailed, damage control required the communication of absolute penitence, a good bit of groveling, apologizing, and swearing that it would never happen again, and above all, the promise that you would be forever tormented by your misbehavior and that no amount of punishment would ever approach the low-life feeling that would haunt you for the rest of your days.

Sarah was sent to Priscilla's friend's house to retrieve her. Ashen-faced, she demanded, "Priscilla, you have to come home right now. You are in *so* much trouble!" Priscilla, at fifteen, had endured ten years of this (we never did it to children under the age of five) and considered herself invincible to our lies. She shrugged, smiled, and retorted, "Yeah, sure." Sarah urgently repeated, "Priscilla, I swear to God you are in *big* trouble. You need to come home." Unfortunately, we had already invoked the name of God and almost anyone else who stood for honesty, goodness, and fairness in our attempts to fool her, so this was worthless. Sarah whispered, "Priscilla, it's about Sacred Heart. Mom knows. She is bullshit! Come home. Now!" Priscilla looked up from what she was doing, nodded, and sarcastically answered, "Right." At that point, Sarah dragged Priscilla to the car and drove her home.

My mother was up in her bedroom, which in times of major infractions became the family courtroom. Chip and I were already situated in the small second-floor bathroom, a great place to hear the action. We weighed the severity of our previous infractions at fifteen (driving without a license and shoplifting) against Priscilla's. Ours were bad because they involved "the law," but were regarded by my parents as impulsive acts, one-time-only stunts (which, of course, they weren't, but we spared them further pain by letting them think they were). Priscilla's crimes were premeditated and repeated. This was virgin territory.

We had no idea what to expect.

Sarah joined us breathlessly in our hiding place, whispering, "She thinks I'm kidding!" This was going to be really interesting. Priscilla took her sweet time emerging from the car. Months of lying had given her a certain confidence I'd never noticed in her before. She sauntered into the house and dawdled at the hall table.

"What the hell is she doing?" demanded Chip.

"Jesus, she's checking the damn mail!" Sarah told him.

"She is dog meat," I concluded, feeling slightly responsible for the impending blowup.

Priscilla yelled up the stairs, "Mom, did you want me?"

"Priscilla, get up here," she yelled back.

We held our breath.

"Get up here" to the rest of us meant "Haul your ass up here." But not to Priscilla. She swaggered up the stairs and walked down the hall, taking her slow, brazen time about it.

"Yeah, Mom?" Priscilla asked.

"What do you mean, 'Yeah, Mom?'?" My mother's voice sounded like she'd been crying.

"How come I had to come home from Molly's?"

"You don't *know?*" my mother answered incredulously. "Isn't there something you haven't been telling me?"

Squeezed into the tiny bathroom together, Chip, Sarah, and I were dying. "Confess, Priscilla, confess," someone whispered.

"I don't think so," answered Priscilla.

"About school?" my mother prompted.

Priscilla was silent. One of us was ready to burst out and offer to represent her in the proceedings since she was doing such a wretched job of defending herself.

"Priscilla, Sister Matthew called today and it became clear that you have been skipping school and writing outlandish excuses. So far, the count is at fifty. They're still checking for the final total." Silence. "What do you have to say for yourself?"

Here it was, the opportunity for groveling, self-flagellation, throwing herself on the mercy of the court.

"Well, Mom," she answered without the slightest bit of remorse, "I *told* you I hated school."

Chip, Sarah, and I were beside ourselves, trying to stay quiet and undetected but mouthing to each other, "Can you *believe* her?" Remembering his unfortunate and illegal driving incident, Chip muttered, "Oh, I get it. I should have said, 'Mom, I *told* you I needed the car.'" I suppressed a laugh and whispered sarcastically about my shoplifting adventures, "Mom, I *told* you I wanted those five records, two lipsticks, and three pairs of earrings."

"Is that *it?*" my mother asked in disbelief.

"Pretty much," answered Priscilla, totally unfazed by the whole thing.

My parents were not into physical punishment. They relied on guilt and grounding. The combination of Priscilla's skipping school, lying about excuses, and then being totally unrepentant and making it almost sound like it was all my mother's fault qualified her for house arrest for the remainder of her adolescence.

The room was silent. It was time for my mother to either yell or proceed directly into guilt induction with the standard "I'm so disappointed in you," said in a way that made you wish she'd just hit you and get it over with. But instead, my mother started asking Priscilla questions about why she hated school and what they could do about it. Skulking in the bathroom, we looked at each other in disbelief. No way was this woman our mother.

They proceeded to have a heart-to-heart talk, in which the worst thing my mother admitted was that it was going to be difficult for her to trust Priscilla for a while. She told her that there would be a conference at school to decide how to help her feel more comfortable.

"*Comfortable?*" my brother hissed. "She wants Priscilla to be *comfortable?* Who is ever *comfortable* at school?"

Sarah and I, who had both endured the full four years at Priscilla's school, were too aghast even to open our mouths.

In addition, we heard my mother tell Priscilla that she would be taking some time out of geometry for the next few weeks to talk to the school psychologist about her "feelings."

Sarah whispered sarcastically, "*Feelings?*" and put her finger down her throat as though she was about to retch.

There was more silence, during which my mother hugged poor, misunderstood, possibly psychologically wounded Priscilla. Priscilla walked out of my mother's room and gently closed the door behind her. We cracked the bathroom door open and whispered to her to come in so we could get the complete lowdown. But she shook her head, gave us the most superior smile I had ever seen, and walked right on by.

✿ NO FAIR

I HAVE ALWAYS found great comfort, wisdom, and challenge in the Holy Scriptures. One of the main messages of the Old and New Testaments affirms that, basically, God or no God, Christ or no Christ, life just isn't fair. It is only in the afterlife that it all evens out. So much of the Bible is essentially the story of the good guys against the bad guys. Like most children, I started out as a fundamentalist, never even entertaining the possibility of Bible stories as metaphors or parables.

I usually found myself on the side of the good guys. I rooted for the poor Israelites as God tested them in their relentless search for home. I loved that Noah eventually found dry land, that Jonah didn't end up lunch meat, and that Sarah got pregnant after seventy-five years of trying. When Moses parted the Red Sea with Pharaoh's army on his ass, it was more exciting than Superman. And when he put the sea back together so that the bad guys drowned, I understood the incredible power of God's backing. When the underdog David knocked the crap out of Goliath, I identified with the little guy and was delighted at his against-all-odds victory.

As my capacity for resentment and enmity grew with age, I could appreciate the way God periodically got fed up with whatever bullshit was going on at the time and pulled out the curses. I especially liked the plagues that God promised and delivered in supporting Moses against the Egyptians. Turning the water of the Nile into blood was pretty gross, but the frogs, flies, gnats, boils, locusts, and darkness were cool. I did think God carried it a bit far, however, with the killing of every firstborn whose family had not marked their door. Perhaps because I am a firstborn, I struggled with the reasons that God would punish innocent children and animals just because their parents screwed up.

And Job, poor Job. God really went over the top on that one. Even though everything turned out all right in the end, Job's downward spiral challenged the "Cheer up . . . It could be worse" method of rationalizing pain. Maybe he was just one incredibly unlucky guy. But maybe it was better not to identify with him too much, I thought, just in case bad luck is contagious.

When Christ kicked the moneylenders out of the temple, I thought, Good move. When he stopped the stoning of an adulterous woman, I was proud. When he continually outfoxed the Pharisees with fancy verbal footwork, I knew I was on the right team. I was sad when he was betrayed and killed and glad when he rose up again.

In all these stories, I rooted for the protagonists. Yet there was this one problematic theme in both the Old and New Testaments that I could never abide. It didn't change with age, insight, or wisdom. It wasn't influenced by schooling or sermons in church. There was one place I identified with the bad guys. It was when God played favorites, *for no good reason,* and the outcomes weren't at all fair.

Why did God look down at Cain, the tiller of the soil, and Abel, the keeper of sheep, and decide that Abel's offering was good and Cain's wasn't? The Bible says, "So Cain was very angry and his countenance fell." Well, of course it did. Whose wouldn't? I'm not saying that it was all right to go ahead and kill Abel or anything, but I understand the motive. When asked where his murdered brother was, Cain delivered the classic, "I don't know. Am I my brother's keeper?" His brother's killer? Yeah, maybe. But definitely not his keeper.

I was my brother's keeper. And I also wanted to kill him. Of course I was only six, so it's not as bad as it sounds. My brother and I came so close in time that we share the same age for one month every year. He was like my second skin, my shadow, following along like a puppy despite my persistence in trying to shoo him away. When I complained to my mother, she would plead, "Martha, he just wants to be with you. Can't you let him play with you for a while?" I loved kindergarten because I got to go and he didn't. But the next September, both of us dressed for school. I was thrilled to be a big first-grader, staying the whole day and learning important stuff like reading and writing rather than the kindergarten playing and sharing that you could do just as well at home. Chip was not at all happy about the prospect of school. As my mother dragged him up the steps of school, I burst ahead and ran to my new classroom, determined that I was not going to be associated with my crybaby brother. But an hour into first grade, a teacher knocked on our classroom door and whispered to my teacher. Then my new teacher asked, "Who is Martha?" I tentatively raised my hand. She motioned me up to the front of the room and handed me over to the other teacher, who just smiled and said, "Follow me." Grown-ups say that kind of stuff as if it's nothing, when it is really scary and confusing to kids. Why was I being taken away? Was it something I did? Something my parents did?

We turned the corner and walked toward the end of the hall where the two kindergarten rooms were. *Oh no! I have to go back to kindergarten.*

I fought against crying because I didn't want them to think I was any more of a baby than they obviously already did. As we got close to my old classroom, I heard crying. Wailing, really. I knew that noise. It was Chip.

The teacher opened the door and said, "We were hoping you could help us with your brother." I didn't see him anywhere, but I could hear him. The teacher pointed to a table, and there was Chip—under it. He sat under the table in his little short pants and blazer. He hadn't even taken off his cap. His wailing turned to whimpering, and he gave me a look like an animal at the pound who knows that if someone doesn't take him soon, he's a goner. I looked up at the two teachers in bewilderment.

"What do you want *me* to do?"

"Get him to come out from under the table."

If they couldn't do it, how was I supposed to?

"But I'm only six years old."

"Yes, dear, we know, but you are his big sister."

I needed to get back to first grade fast, so I crawled under the table and demanded that he come out. He shook his head. I pulled his arm. He weighed more than I did. I pleaded with him to come out. He refused. All the while I'm trying to ease him out, the teachers are bending over and saying, "Come on, Chuck, it's okay, Chuck . . . Just come on out. No one will hurt you, Chuck." Every time they called him "Chuck," he burst into a new round of tears. Things were getting worse, not better. I despaired of ever returning to first grade.

"His name's not Chuck!" I yelled. "It's Chip."

They struck a deal with Chip that I would stay for a while if he came out from under the table. My first-grade time was being sacrificed for his kindergarten.

I had planned to learn how to read on that first day, and he screwed it all up. Chip spent the first quarter of kindergarten under that table. But after that first day, I resigned from being my brother's keeper. He became my mother's problem, not mine. I had bigger things to deal with.

Another story that always got to me was Jesus' parable of the vineyard owner. The workers who showed up only an hour before quitting time were paid the exact same wages as those who'd worked the entire day. Naturally, the guys who'd been sweating it

Chasing Grace

out all day protested to the vineyard owner about the unfairness of it all. Why should someone who came late and did next to nothing receive the same wages as those who worked a full day? The vineyard owner asks the unhappy full-day workers if he has paid them according to their agreement. They grudgingly agree. Then he tells them basically that what he gives to someone else is no one else's damn business. I could always picture those full-day guys at a loss for any words except "Yeah, but . . ."

I was invited to Allen Francis's seven-year birthday party down the street. Only kids my age were invited. Chip was devastated because he couldn't go. I was so pleased because it was one of the few times that nobody could say, "Oh, go on, Martha, just let him go with you." I got all dressed up for the party. It was really fun. We played pin-the-tail-on-the-donkey and I won. Right before the cake, the doorbell rang, and it was Chip—standing there with his freckled face smushed up against the window, his dirty cheeks covered with tears, his shoes and clothes filthy from playing in the mud. I told Allen's mother, "Just shut the door. He'll go away. My mother explained to him all about how you can't go where you aren't invited." But Allen's mother said, "Oh no, it's okay," as she opened the door for dirty Chip, who looked ecstatic. He gratefully took the punch and the cake, and Allen's mother slobbered about how cute he was. I hated him.

As a pilot for American Airlines, Allen's father had gotten really cool captain's wings as party favors. They looked just like the real thing. As he handed them out, he pinned them on each kid and they beamed with their wings in place. Except when it came my turn, I got a stupid stewardess pin. It was round and small and didn't look like anything important. And then my totally presumptuous brother held out his fat, filthy little hand and Mr. Francis pinned the captain's wings on his chest. I didn't think it was possible, but I hated him even more.

❧ MY BABY BOOK

THE TITLE of my baby book is "Our Baby's First Seven Years." My first year was documented by my mother with the attention of an anthropological observer; she packed twenty pages with sixty-six captioned photographs, the family tree, cards and telegrams, milestone charts, and narrative. The next six years are filled with thirty-five pages of nothing.

The verbal and pictorial history of my childhood begins with a letter to my father from his boss, J. Edgar Hoover, otherwise known as "The Director," on one page and the notice of my birth in the Saint James Catholic Church bulletin on the other. There is something a bit unsettling about the fact that the first pieces of mail related to me came from the Department of Justice and the Holy Roman Catholic Church.

Hoover's note was benign, which makes me believe that someone else probably wrote it and he only lent his signature: "May I offer my hearty congratulations . . . upon the arrival of your daughter, Martha Mary. I know that your little girl has brightened both of your lives and it is my sincere wish that happiness and good health will be with her always." Given the rule that FBI agents were expected to report any negative interactions that their "little girls and boys" had with the law, which then resulted in punitive transfers to remote places, I'm surprised he didn't wish me a clean record as well.

The Catholic announcement made no promises, threats, or wishes. It simply noted my full name, the date of my baptism, and my parents' names and address. The announcement of my baptism was positioned across from even bigger features in the parish bulletin:

The drive-through wash rack at the Second Avenue Mobil Service Station is now open from 9 AM to 2 PM on Sundays.

You can leave your car there while you come to church, and pick it up after Mass, sparkling like new.

and

There are still warm days ahead on the calendar. . . . Don't forget that the Forestview Liquor Store will furnish you with all the ice cubes you wish free of charge. The store also will lend punch bowls and cups, cocktail glasses and highball glasses for parties.

In addition, there was a lengthy discussion of how to recruit "NON-Catholics" into the fold. Titled "How good a salesman are you?" it recommends that Catholics knock on people's doors and say, "You know we Catholics have acquired rather a bad reputation for being clannish. We would like to correct that." Neighbors are then invited to "inquiry classes" about "the faith." A recruiter is encouraged to "Be an apostle and spread the faith by getting behind this movement, and giving it all you've got. You can be the cause of someone saving their soul."

The description of my life begins on page three, where my mother chronicled the events in my life as if I were writing about them myself. Before I could do anything but gurgle and howl, my mother provided me with a voice and a style. As I flip through the faded blue pages, filled with my mother's seamless Palmer-method longhand, written in the same blue cartridge-pen ink, I compare what appears on each page with what was left out, knowing that what is absent from a story is often at least as significant as what is there.

THE STORY: PART ONE

"My name is Martha Mary Manning. This is my story. I was born at 3:40 PM on August 18, 1952 at the Wesley Memorial Hospital in Chicago, Illinois. I then came to live at 347 Indianwood Blvd., Park Forest, Illinois with my Mommy and Daddy and our dog Midget. I weighed 8 lbs 3 oz when I was born and 7 lbs 6 oz when I came home."

The Story Behind the Story

I was born nine months and one day after my parents were married. My conception most likely occurred at the Greenbrier Resort in White Sulphur Springs, West Virginia, on what my mother refers to as "the dumbest honeymoon in the world." The honeymoon would be the first and last time my father was allowed to exclusively plan the itinerary for anything but the trips he took alone.

My parents drove from their wedding reception in Boston to a supposedly charming hotel in Wappingers Falls, New York, that turned out to be a local Saturday-night hangout. Apparently, the joint was jumping, with a band in every room downstairs—not exactly the bucolic wedding night my parents had expected.

From there, they drove to West Virginia. At some point during this leg of the trip, they ran out of gas, dealt with two flat tires, and had their first big fight. It was one of the worst kinds of fights—the "car fight." You're stuck in close proximity to the person you thought you loved, but now really hate, and you can't get away from each other. All your usual ways of ending arguments, like yelling, "Screw you!" and exiting loudly with a satisfying slam of a door, aren't advisable, unless you are so angry that you're willing to put your life in jeopardy just to make a point.

Once they arrived at the Greenbrier Resort, my father fully expected that my mother would be as interested in horseback riding as he was. Apparently, this was another thing that had not been discussed before the honeymoon. My mother refused, insisting that her head was the only part of her body that had not yet been broken and she preferred to keep it that way. My father rode alone and my mother walked around a lot. From there, they traveled to Williamsburg, Virginia, where they celebrated a lovely

Thanksgiving and agree that it almost made up for everything else.

When they arrived at their brand-new house in Cleveland several days later, they found that their furniture would not arrive for another week. So they slept on laundry. "We started our married life the way it's always been," my mother recounts. And it's true. So much about my parents' life together is embodied in those days. My father's grand plans are often much better in fantasy than in reality. The basic differences in their temperaments and interests mean that my father's dreams are always battling my mother's practicality.

My mother and father didn't know each other very well before they were married. And they were not a married couple very long before I came on the scene. They also didn't have much of a chance to "settle down," because after only months in Cleveland, my father was transferred to Chicago.

When it appeared that my birth was imminent, my parents had another major car fight. This one was over who was going to drive the forty-five minutes to the hospital. My father had an acute eye infection that seriously compromised his vision in one eye. My mother insisted that even with her contractions, she had a better shot at getting us all to the hospital alive. But my father prevailed, and drove half-blind to the hospital. My mother's doctor took one look at my mother, another at my father, and pronounced my father in greater need of immediate attention. He sent him off to the emergency room and dispatched my mother to labor and delivery.

I did not enter the world gracefully. As has been true of most of my life, I made it about as difficult on myself (not to mention my mother) as it could possibly get. Having been a silent party to the first year of my parents' life together, during which they smoothed over some of their early rough edges, maybe I wasn't quite ready to jump into the fray. And if I'd had any doubts before, the ride to the hospital would have only confirmed my ambivalence about coming out.

The medical term for the way in which I chose to present myself is "posterior presentation," which means that I was positioned facedown rather than faceup. Faceup is by far the preferred method of delivery because the shoulders can turn inward to ease the baby through the birth canal. But I was, as I often still am, looking down. They did everything but dynamite me out. The doctor had to push me back in, turn me around, and then pull me out. I cooperated with none of this. My mother required a transfusion and more than one hundred stitches, or, as the obstetrician explained to my father, "embroidery on her differential."

I looked so bad after delivery that my parents took one pained glance and rejected the pictures routinely taken in the hospital nursery. My face was cut and bruised from forceps. My head was tremendously misshapen, my nose was pressed flat across my face from cheekbone to cheekbone (later it was determined that it had been broken), and I was beet red. When I was handed to my mother for the first time, she looked at her little eight-pound bundle of wailing ugliness and exclaimed, "All that for *this?*" Shortly after my birth, my parents called their families in Boston to announce my arrival. They must have emphasized the ugly part a bit too much, because my grandmother became immediately concerned about "genetic" problems and was convinced that, at the very least, I was mentally retarded. She alerted as many people as she knew, as well as a good number she didn't, to pray for me.

My mother and the nurses worked on my nose for several days and it started shaping up. The cuts and bruises healed, and I began to have the beginnings of a human head. After five days, my very sore mother and I were allowed to go home. When the nurse wheeled us to the front door where my father was waiting, he greeted us with a brand-new car—a small item he had neglected to tell my mother about during our stay, and something we could not afford. I spent my very first hour with my new family listening to a car fight.

The next entry in my baby book is about my christening and general life during my first few weeks.

"Three weeks after I was born, I went to church for the first time and officially became Martha Mary. They tell me I behaved quite well at the christening in spite of the fact that I had on my great-grandfather's christening dress which had yards of skirt, and several petticoats. My godparents are my Aunt Nancy and my Uncle Frank. Afterwards we had a little party. Everyone toasted me and I slept peacefully through most of the festivities.

"My first weeks I did nothing but eat and sleep and Mommy tells me that Daddy couldn't wait for me to get old enough to play with. When I was three weeks old I had my first cereal and loved it. At four weeks I started mashed banana and when I was two months old I started on three meals a day and oh, do I love to eat!

"In October I took my first long trip—to Boston to visit all of my aunts and uncles, my grandmothers and grandfather, and my three great-grandparents. It was so much fun because everyone played with me. By this time I had learned how to smile and practiced on everyone. It was such fun to meet everyone I had heard so much about."

The Story Behind the Story

By October, only two months after my birth, my mother was pregnant again. At this news, my father's mother, who would usually never address such matters, mentioned something to my father about pacing himself. Our trip to Boston was filled with all the attention that the firstborn child and first grandchild usually get. Being at the front of the line versus the back was significant.

By the time the twentieth grandchild arrived, the excitement had died down considerably. Sometimes, the most attention the last few kids got was, "What was your name again?" But I was passed like a treasure from one person to the next and proclaimed beautiful, sunny, and—after a careful once-over followed by a quick prayer of thanksgiving—smart.

My presence redeemed my father in the eyes of some relatives who had been exceedingly disappointed when he abandoned his quest for Catholic priesthood and married my mother. Even the ones who hadn't spoken to him now had something to say, at least to me, and by association, to him. We returned to Illinois, where my father lived the life of a tremendously overworked FBI agent and my mother took care of me and advanced in her second pregnancy. She remained a faithful diarist on my behalf, and in her writing she begins to acknowledge a growing separateness between us.

THE STORY: PART THREE

"In June, when I was nine and a half months old I started to stand in the playpen and really creep around the house. All of a sudden, I started moving on my knees and going like lightning. There were so many things to pull at and examine that I'm afraid I kept Mommy chasing after me. When she doesn't want me to touch, she says 'No' in a very stern voice and then slaps my hand if I don't stop. This hurts, so I keep away from things when she says 'No,' most of the time anyway.

"The first word I tried to say was 'Midg,' but all I could manage at first was 'a-dga.' I also tried very hard to say 'hi,' but nothing came out, so I would just open my mouth wide and pretend. I can pat-a-cake and wave bye-bye, although I get them mixed up and do the wrong thing at the wrong time. Learning new things can be so confusing.

"I also have quite a mind of my own and when Mommy would try to feed me something I didn't like or wasn't hungry for

I would push the food away so quickly that the food would spill all over everything and then Mommy would get mad at me. Sometimes she would play a game while I was eating and would put some food in my mouth when I wasn't looking. But soon I learned that I could spit it right out, so I was always covered with a huge lobster bib."

The Story Behind the Story

It was clear that my parents were delighted to see the emergence of my strong will but also found it a bit wearing. I was, by all accounts, always moving. Even seated on my mother's lap, I squirmed, rocked, wriggled, and bounced. This may have been partially influenced by the fact that my mother was prescribed Dexedrine during her entire pregnancy. In every home movie, I look like my central nervous system is still hopped up on speed. My father reports that I had a habit of drinking a bottle in my crib and, when finished, standing up and chucking it onto the floor. Bottles were made of glass in those days, and our house was built on a slab. I was delighted to learn that bottles, when tossed with enough energy, could crash and explode on the floor. My parents would be relaxing, enjoying their first fifteen minutes of peace and quiet, when there would be a crash, followed by squeals of laughter. They were totally unsuccessful at getting me to stop, and I firmly refused to sleep without a bottle. They finally found a cushion they could wrap around my bottles, which allowed me to have the milk but deprived me, at least temporarily, of the great joy of throwing things.

By the time I was nine and a half months old, my mother was seven and a half months pregnant. As I was becoming more active, my mother was becoming more tired—particularly as she faced the prospect of another baby so soon. It was becoming clear that my father would be allowed only the most minimal time off for my brother's birth. They couldn't afford a nurse or baby-sitter, and no one from Boston was able to travel to Chicago to care for me. I was, however, invited for a six-week visit to my grandparents at their beach house in Scituate, Massachusetts, so that my mother could get some rest before my brother's birth and then have some time to settle in with him afterward. My parents quickly accepted.

THE STORY: PART FOUR

"My vacation trip. On July 10th I started for Boston all by myself without Mommy and Daddy. A friend of Mommy and Daddy's who was a stewardess took me into a big big plane and the next thing I knew I was waking up in New York with Grandmother Cooney to meet me. She took me in the car to Scituate, which is just the most wonderful place ever. It has all the sand in the world just lying on the ground for miles and so much water that you can't see where it ends. I am always good, so of course I was good on my first vacation even though I got so much attention from my grandmother and grandfather, great-grandmothers and -fathers and aunts and uncles.

"After I had been in Scituate for a while, Grandmother told me one day that Mommy and Daddy had just bought me a new baby brother and a little while later showed me a picture of him. His real name is John, my parents call him Chip. I don't care what anyone calls him. I think he's cute.

"Everyone was so wonderful to me so that I almost forgot about Mommy and Daddy. I had my first birthday and had the nicest party with all the children in the neighborhood. Eating the gumdrops off the cake was the most fun. Later on, Mommy and Daddy brought Chip to me. He is lots of fun. He just lies there but I kiss him and pat him and I just love him. I'm so glad that Mommy and Daddy gave me such a nice playmate and I can hardly wait till he gets a little older and I can really play with him.

"I started to walk in Boston—a few steps at a time—and by the time I was back in Chicago, within two weeks I was going all over the house. I also said my first word in Scituate, 'Duck,' and by the time I was fourteen months old I could say 'Hi' and tried to say 'Kitty' but all that comes out is 'K-K.'"

The Story Behind the Story

My baby book ends right there. For years, the story of me at ten and a half months getting on a night plane to New York was almost mythic. I loved to hear my grandmother and my parents tell the story. The emphasis was always on the wonderful adventure of it all. How they all spoiled me when I got to the beach house. The adorable dresses and bonnets. The endless studio photos. The wonderful birthday party. Being wheeled up and down the street by my proud grandfather, a gruff, hardworking man who probably never wheeled his own children anywhere. Learning about the sand and discovering my early and lasting love of the ocean. Sitting naked in my favorite "playpen"—a dory dragged up from the beach to the seawall, filled with enough frigid Atlantic water to give me the illusion I was in the ocean, but shallow enough that I couldn't drown.

In the pictures and the home movies I see a beautiful, thriving baby with white hair and brown skin, with her new little Chiclets teeth widely spaced in delighted smiles, always rocking, moving, and splashing, being handed around in a continuous circle between the great-grandmother, grandmother, aunts and uncles, and baby-sitters.

It wasn't until I had my own child and we approached the age at which my parents sent me to my grandparents that I began to reinterpret the version of the story in the baby book. The word *vacation* rang false. Vacation for whom? I couldn't bear the thought of being separated from my daughter for her first steps, her first words, her first birthday. And I couldn't even *guess* what impact that kind of separation would have had on her.

"Why did you send me to Boston?" I grilled my mother.

"Because we had no one else to take care of you and no money."

"But how did you *feel?*" I asked, hoping for pain.

"Mixed," she answered. "It was lovely to have time to myself. You know I don't really get attached to babies. I would have missed you much more when you were older."

Not exactly what I was looking for.

"But in the part of you that did miss me, what did you think?"

"Well, I thought, This is my time and my child is being well cared for."

"But what was it like to miss my first birthday?"

"Martha, you *know* I'm a pragmatic person. I just thought, Well, I'll be there on her second birthday."

"But how did *I* react when I saw you after six weeks?" I pressed.

"You weren't wildly excited. It took a little while for you to come to me. You were so attached to Grandmother. But you came. And you surprised everyone by how well you got along with Chip. It was always surprising to us how little jealousy you showed toward him."

"What was it like when the four of us got home?"

"It was a blur . . . the whole of your growing up was a blur to me. I had the six of you with absolutely no help. And there was always one or more of you sick. Whenever we moved someplace new, the first person I met was the doctor, the second was the druggist."

My one and only baby is now seventeen. I think I understand why my baby book ended as it did. My brother's baby book, which looked exactly the same on the outside, lasted for only one month and a scant five pages. Then the "blur" settled in for years and dramatically changed my mother's life and mine. The next four children didn't even have baby books. They had a bottom drawer in a dining-room cabinet into which photos, report cards, letters, and drawings were tossed. Years later, when we root around in the pictures, long discussions begin with, "Whose baby picture is this?" and sometimes end with claims that cannot be totally supported or denied by my parents. Unlike the careful charting of the date and position of my every new tooth, and every other developmental milestone, about the only thing my parents can tell the rest of their children about their development is that eventually they all walked, talked, and got teeth.

But I never felt a bit sorry for my brothers and sisters. They were in the enviable position of not knowing what they'd missed. Only I knew. Of the six of us, I had the shortest time as "the baby." Sometimes I wonder if it's the reason I waited seven years for a second child, wanting to give my daughter the same abundance of attention and love that my parents gave me—but to let her have it all to herself for much, much longer. Throughout my life, I have sometimes been seduced into resentful memories of having to share life in the "blur" with so many other people. I have fumed with the unanswerable questions that begin "Why didn't they?" or "How could they?" But seventeen years of motherhood have made me more humble and taught me that love can't be measured in units of undivided attention.

I remember being truly surprised when, at fifteen, I returned from a weeklong student-council camp to a very unhappy mother. "You never called or wrote to us," she said, her voice registering more hurt than my mother usually displayed.

"You knew where I was," I replied casually, assuming that she was angry that I hadn't checked in.

"I missed you," she said above the noise of a bunch of kids tripping over one another to greet me at the front door.

"*Me?*" I asked, not sure I'd heard her right.

"Yes, *you*. Of course, *you*," she yelled over the din. "I wanted to know about how you liked it, how it was going."

I was totally surprised. I didn't believe anybody would *notice*, let alone *miss*, one kid out of six for a week. But the look on my mother's face made me believe her. She hadn't just missed me, the deputy mother. She had missed me, the fifteen-year-old full of contrary opinions and attitude and an unmasked disdain for almost every aspect of my parents' ideas, appearance, and behavior. She missed the real me.

Having a child of my own initially raised disturbing questions about my relationship with my parents, and then later quieted many of those same concerns. I fully realized how hard it is to raise just one child, and I marveled that my parents didn't just run away from the six of us in the middle of the night—or sell us all to the circus. I also had to own up to the fact that while my daughter never had to share me with other children, she had a more formidable competitor—my ambition, which drove me to try to accomplish too many things at one time. As I righteously complain about being eclipsed by younger children, my daughter vehemently protests being enrolled in what I now see was a lousy after-school day-care program. All she wanted, she tells me and will tell me for the rest of my life, was to come directly home after what was already a long day of school. When I see my baby book end after only one year, I remember my daughter's almost empty baby book. At that time, I was saving all my words for my dissertation.

The contents of the baby books and bureau drawers documenting the progress of the life of my whole family have spilled over onto my parents' refrigerators and freezers, invaded the corners of mirrors, and laid claim to every empty space in their already full house. They clutter my parents' desks and form collages of Manning generations. Grandchildren's report cards and pipe-cleaner-and-paper-plate constructions share magnets with my brother's award from hairdressing school, next to a writing award I won last year, under letters of commendation for major deals my brother or sister have made. Another sister's clever faxes are affixed to memos about scheduled birthday parties and holiday chores already assigned by my organized mother. There are yellowing smart-ass notes and cartoons from all of us.

Our children peek in and out of our papers, with their hockey and lacrosse sticks, violins and flutes, report cards, drawings and poems, and faces that change with each year's school pictures. There is no better proof of "the blur" than in the corners and surfaces of my parents' house. But there is also no better proof that while attention is often divided, love sustains an amazing capacity to multiply.

✤ SIN

WHEN I REACHED the sweet age of seven, the church determined me capable of recognizing, registering, reporting, and repenting my sins. Several days before my first holy communion I was scheduled to receive the sacrament of penance to confess my sins. First confession was nowhere near as big a deal as first communion. No one gave me gifts for admitting publicly that I was a sinner. No one made me a cake that said HAPPY PENANCE. First confession was like the regular Saturday-night bath as a requisite for church on Sunday morning. A bath for your soul.

Even though it wasn't celebrated with the pomp and ceremony of first communion, the sacrament of penance required tremendous preparation.

You had to start with the basic Judeo-Christian sins as outlined in the Ten Commandments. Some of them were hard to understand. We spent hours going over the nuances of "Honor thy father and mother," but when Robert McFadden asked Sister Miriam Jerome exactly what "coveting thy neighbor's wife" meant, she glared at him and admonished him not to be "fresh" so close to first communion, because it wasn't too late for him to be "taken off the list." I understood that coveting was something like wanting. But why would my father "covet" Mrs. Whalen next door or Mrs. Ryan down the street? It didn't take long to figure out that you didn't really have to *understand* the sins; you just had to remember them and, above all else, spell them correctly.

After the Judeo-Christian sins came the Catholic sins, which were considerably more complicated and, given the attention they received in our preparation, considerably more important. Sins were differentiated by severity: venial (bad, but not too terrible—like hitting your older brother) and mortal (the express route to hell—like hitting a priest or a nun). To illustrate this distinction to children, our catechism depicted three milk bottles representing our souls. Soul Number One was unblemished and perfectly white, looking exactly like the stuff that was delivered each morning to our doorstep and that we were made to drink to the last drop as a precondition for dessert. This was the picture of our souls in a state of grace—plain old white milk. Soul Number Two with its venial sins had dark spots against a background of white, vaguely suggesting chocolate chips. Soul Number Three, engulfed by mortal sin, was totally dark, looking like what Mary Catherine Lawson had when her mother (unlike mine) allowed her to pour large quantities of Hershey's syrup into unappealing white milk. Needless to say, the chocolate milk was the clear favorite to me, which probably explains a great deal about my subsequent spiritual and moral development.

Second grade marked the beginning of years of what-if questions posed to priests and nuns for the purpose of testing the absolute boundaries of sin. There were numerous rules about attendance at mass, holy days, Friday abstinence from meat, and fasting. For every rule, we plagued our teachers with every possible exception. In the fasting domain: "Sister, what if you have this really, really bad cough and your mother was supposed to give you your cough medicine by midnight, but she didn't get home until three minutes after midnight and she made you take it anyway. Can you still go to communion?" Answer: "Our Lord understands that these things can happen. If anyone is at fault, it is your mother. You may receive the Eucharist." In the "never touch yourself" domain: "But Father, what if you were in the woods and you got bitten by a very unusual bug and you had a terrible, awful itch and you thought you would go crazy if you didn't reach down and scratch it?" Answer: "Well, you may scratch it to relieve the suffering caused by the bug bite and still remain in a state of grace— as long as there is no pleasure experienced in the act."

Because I moved into the parish after kindergarten, I had to attend public school while moving up on the waiting list for Our

Lady Queen of Angels school. I prepared for the sacraments on Sunday mornings with Sister Miriam Jerome. She was a little bulldog of a woman, solid and tough, with the voice of a New Jersey trucker. She paced up and down the aisles swinging her long rosary beads with an authority that suggested she could pick off a misbehaving student with them in a split second. It took some getting used to after first grade with Sister Mary Ambrose, who gave us old candy and holy cards that portrayed a Caucasian, hippie-looking Jesus happily surrounded by little children. She told us how "wondrously" we were made and how much God loved us. My first hour of second grade made it clear that first grade was just recruitment. Second grade was boot camp.

The emphasis was no longer on the "I'm okay, you're okay" message from God. Now God was telling us, "I'm okay. You definitely aren't, and I've got my eye on you."

This was the wrathful God who had either a really good memory or some excellent accountants to monitor your every move. In that way, God became like Santa Claus, still essentially benign, but always waiting for you to screw up, with the threat of dire consequences forever in the air. "He sees you when you're sleeping. He knows when you're awake . . ."

Second grade was also my first exposure to a particular kind of Catholic sin: nun sin. While pissing off a nun was not *technically* on any sin list, the displeasure and the consequences of transgressing one of the many rules within the nuns' classroom kingdom seemed much worse than any other kind of hell. Sister Miriam Jerome must have taken years to finesse her list of rules. They were pronounced as if she were reading from a tablet personally presented to her on Mount Sinai. Moving your desk one millimeter off the taped edges on the floor made her furious. Folding your hands incorrectly when you prayed (left thumb is always to be placed over right thumb) made her near-homicidal.

But the worst one was the envelope commandment. She had a rule that if you were absent from class, you were required to bring a note from your parents. It had to be in a letter-sized envelope. The envelope had to be unsealed. It could not have any writing on the front or the back. Following an absence the week before, I reminded my father several times that I needed a note. I outlined the parameters of the contents and the crucial envelope rules. That night he presented me with the note. Instantly I knew it was unacceptable. It was in a legal-sized envelope. On the front of it he had written, "Most Reverend Sister Miriam Jerome." And, as if that weren't enough, it was sealed.

"Dad, this note is all wrong."

"What do you mean it's wrong?"

"You didn't follow the envelope rules," I told him with alarm.

I thought that having had the error of his ways pointed out would make him leap up immediately to correct it. He didn't. He shrugged and said that he had written a perfectly nice letter and that my teacher would be very happy with it. I tried to tell him about the size, writing, and licking rules, all of which he'd transgressed. "Don't worry about it, Marth. It'll be fine."

Fine? I thought. Fine? He of all people should know that it's not "fine" when you break the rules. He almost became a priest. He should know about these rules. But he wouldn't change it.

I stayed up all night in dread of Sunday school. It was the kind of dread for which there is no comfort. You are standing in the middle of the street and when rush hour comes, you know with absolute certainty that you will be flattened by a truck. No outs. No maybes. You just have to wait out the sentence of time before what is dreaded finally becomes what is real.

I crept into her classroom that Sunday morning weak from a combination of fasting and terror. When she collected the absentee notes, I presented mine last, closing my eyes and wincing as she reviewed the awful envelope and its contents. When she finished, she looked up at me. She was flushed and I was sure I was dead meat. But then she beamed. "Please thank your father for this lovely note," she said, motioning for me to take my seat. She

Chasing Grace

gazed at the note for several moments longer. In that small space of time, she lost her pug face and her threatening stance. She looked softer somehow, almost human. Then very carefully, she returned the note to its envelope and tucked it deep within the folds of her habit as if it were a hundred-dollar bill.

I didn't get it. I didn't get that, as opposed to the priests, the nuns were poor and had to be ingenious even to get paper for their personal use. But more than that, I didn't get that nuns did the greatest amount of work and got the least amount of appreciation. I didn't understand that my father's respectful acknowledgment of "Most Reverend Sister Miriam Jerome" would be worth far more to her than any virginal envelope. My father broke the envelope rule, but from Sister's reaction, he had done a good thing. The best thing. It would be a long time before I understood that breaking a rule was different from committing a sin.

✳ HELL

TO MAKE SIN at all relevant to us children, the nuns spent a great deal of time sharpening our imagery skills as we were encouraged to try to imagine hell. To imagine fire beyond the worst burn you've had, to imagine loneliness beyond the worst isolation you have known. To imagine the worst of the worst of the worst, and even then, to know that you haven't gotten one-millionth of the picture of how bad hell is. The other key idea for the seven-year-old mind to grasp was the concept of eternity— forever and ever and ever. I would lie awake at night and do what my teacher had assigned—think about infinity, the endlessness within endlessness of it, the no-second-chances of it, the no-time-off-for-good-behavior of it.

Not only was there hell to worry about, there was also this place called Purgatory, where almost everyone spent some time. If you weren't condemned to hell, but hadn't yet earned your ticket to heaven, you served time in Purgatory. My teachers never helped me to understand the geography of Purgatory. The closest I ever got in my mind was the Greyhound bus station, where we went to pick up my great-aunt Marnie from Boston. It was dark and damp there, and everyone looked dirty and awful. I remember yawning and waiting for my aunt to arrive, checking to see if each bus was hers, and slumping back in my seat upon seeing that it wasn't. I fought with a decrepit candy machine that took my ten cents and gave me nothing, and my mother, not understanding the unfairness of it all, wouldn't give me any more change because I had "squandered" my first dime. The clock just kept ticking, and the people kept dragging their shabby selves and their shabby baggage, coughing and clearing their throats and spitting. I tried to decide which smelled worse, the bus terminal or the bus fumes. I remember asking my mother if I could wait outside because I determined that the bus fumes smelled better. My mother kept saying, "Sit still and be patient." That was Purgatory.

There was also this place called Limbo, for little babies who died before they were baptized. The nuns assured us that no one was mean to them in Limbo, that they were well taken care of. But you had the idea that they were well taken care of in the hospital-nursery kind of way rather than the at-home-snuggling-with-people-who-love-you kind of way.

After they were sure that we had registered all the bad news, the nuns sprung us with the good news. There were actually some ways out of this mess. There was confession, first of all, which wiped the slate clean with whatever frequency (preferably weekly) that you saw fit. Then there were things called indulgences, which were basically Purgatory Parole. You performed the indulgences and earned a specific number of days or years off your sentence to Purgatory. No one ever specified whether our time dimensions were the same as God's or different, like the way we measure human years and dog years. But it was a chance for time off, so who cared?

You got time off from Purgatory by making the sign of the cross, which earned you three years—seven years if you used holy water. Repeating holy phrases (ejaculations) qualified for all kinds of reprieves, although it was hard for me to imagine that when my mother yelled, "JE-sus, Ma-RY, and JO-seph! Didn't I tell you kids not to swing from the railing!" she was actually accumulating grace. Recitation of the rosary would take five years off your sentence—seven years if you recited it in October. Special prayers, such as the Prayer to Saint Joseph in Time of Need, were very complicated. You got three years off for saying it on an average day. But if you said it during the month of October, or with the rosary, or on any Wednesday throughout the year, you hit the jackpot with a seven-year indulgence.

❧ FIRST CONFESSION

THE ACTUAL FIRST CONFESSION would have been anticlimactic to the months of preparation had I not made two major errors. When it came my turn, Sister Miriam Jerome motioned toward the empty confessional box on the right side of Father Moran. I pulled back the heavy green-velvet curtain and knelt on the squeaky rubber-coated kneeler. My face hardly reached the door that the priest slides back to hear your sins. The kid on the left side either had a lot of sins or had forgotten the routine in his anxiety, because he was taking forever. Finally the priest pulled back the small door that separated us. Now there was only a light screen between us. He was slumped in his seat, with his ear turned to me. I saw the shadow of his head and his hand against the wall. I was probably the fiftieth first confession he had heard that day. Strong in my memory, I began, "Bless me, Father, for I have sinned. This is my first confession." When he asked me my sins, I recited them confidently, each sin and its frequency memorized all week and practiced on my little sisters.

"Disobeyed my parents—eight times; fought with my brothers and sisters—six times; used a swear word—one time; lied—two times; committed adultery—four times; diso—"

"What?" he bellowed, loud enough for everyone outside to hear him. "*What* did you do?"

"I disobeyed my teach—" I repeated.

"No," he interrupted impatiently. "Before that."

"Oh, I committed adultery four times."

He started laughing but tried to make it sound like he was coughing one of those I-smoke-too-much kind of coughs. I had no idea what was so funny. "What makes you think you committed adultery?" he wheezed.

"Well, I don't exactly know what it is, but I pretend I'm a grown-up a lot, so I figured that must be it."

"Well, it's not. You won't be eligible for the sin of adultery for a long time. Now for your penance, say five Our Fathers and five Hail Marys and make a good act of contrition."

The act of contrition is a long prayer that the penitent says after each confession as the priest gives absolution. I was so proud that I remembered it.

The first line, the second line. On and on I went. It was almost over. I would never have to go through a first confession again. I got to the part where you promise to stay away from the "*near* occasion of sin," but I must have heard Sister wrong because I thought it was supposed to be the "*dear* occasion of sin" and said so, loud and clear.

"Whose class are you in?" he bellowed.

"Sister Miriam Jerome's, Father."

"What school do you go to?" he demanded.

"Burke Street School, Father."

"Oh, you go to *public* school. That explains a lot," he said disdainfully, as if public school were a den of thieves or a house of prostitution.

"Yes, Father." I responded weakly. I was humiliated. I had just screwed up the sacrament devoted to screwing up. I was seven years old. There was so much I didn't know.

❧ THE BIG M

RECEIVING THE SACRAMENT of penance was just the beginning of my education about guilt and sin. With each year it seemed that my potential as a major sinner was increasing. I found out that I was guilty of infractions that I didn't even know were sins. Gradually, I became aware that there were things I had been doing almost my whole life that were actually grave offenses. Most of these behaviors were in the category of "impurity," which I was to learn much later was the euphemism for any concept or word related to sex.

Around fourth grade, the nuns started talking about self-abuse and what a terrible, horrible thing it was, "a slap in the face to Jesus dying on the cross." I could understand that. I thought self-abuse was pretty bad, too. For two years I'd had a subscription to the Saint of the Month book club. I pored over those books, relishing the romantic suffering of the holy young women I read about. But it often seemed to me that they carried things a bit too far. They engaged in acts of self-mortification: beating themselves with reeds until they bled, walking on glass, painfully constricting their chests and stomachs, fasting for days. These women did not just cheerfully suffer the trials that life deals out to everyone; they went out of their way to be miserable. They rejoiced in it. It wasn't that I hadn't tried to adopt the self-mortification of the saints. I just wasn't very good at it. My fasting never lasted past lunchtime. I tried beating my back with a branch from the rosebush in the front yard, loaded with about three tiny thorns. But those little suckers really hurt and I never got even close to what anyone could call "rapture."

I found myself in total agreement with the church on the issue of "self-abuse." It was definitely not a good idea. But then it became clear that beating yourself up was *not* the kind of self-abuse they were talking about. That stuff was fine. If it hurt, it must be good for you. No, the self-abuse to which they were referring had to do with finding and making liberal use of what Alice Walker called "the secret of joy." The "big M"—masturbation, which was never referred to by name. "Touching yourself" was as close as they got to actually naming the sin.

This was very bad news for a nine-year-old who had discovered "the secret of joy" years before and never lost it. I realized with horror that I was triply guilty. So pleased had I been with my discovery that I had told two of my younger sisters about it. I could understand that lying, stealing, killing, even disobeying your parents were sins, but I just couldn't believe that something that felt so good and harmed no one could be so bad. If God didn't want us to masturbate, why were we given hands that can so effortlessly reach our genitals? Despite the nuns' horror stories with generic themes like "little Johnny touches himself, really likes it, gets distracted, and gets hit by a car," I opted for sin. If that was what they wanted to call it, fine. But for me, masturbation was the closest I ever got to the rapture described in my Saint of the Month books. And it didn't hurt.

The priests in the confessional boxes were keeping up with us developmentally. If you didn't spontaneously mention committing "impure thoughts and deeds," the priest often asked directly if you had anything to confess in that area. This put me in a terrible bind, which I finally resolved by denying to the priest that I had done anything impure and then adding one more to the number of lies I had told that week. In that way, I converted masturbation to lying and was absolved of all my sins.

In the winter of fourth grade, a routine eye exam determined that I had shown a dramatic deterioration over the past year. I was terrified at the news. The nuns were right. I was going blind. Could everyone tell by looking at me? Was this some kind of litmus test for "self-abuse"? Sensing my distress, the ophthalmologist told me that children often started wearing glasses at this time. Yeah, I wanted to say to him. And what do you think they all have in common? He started telling me that many of his patients wore glasses and were "still popular." This guy was totally out of his depth. There he was trying to allay my fears of becoming a geek, while I was wrestling with a future of blindness and the eternal fires of hell.

On the way home, I vowed to give it up, for good. At night, in bed, I tried counting backward to get to sleep. I sang "One hundred bottles of beer on the wall," softly so I wouldn't wake my sisters. I made lists, such as the ten people I would most like to meet and what I would say to them. I thought about Jesus bleeding and dying on the cross for my sins. I thought about hell. But I always caved in, promising that I'd give it another shot the next day. In the case of this sin, I made my first exception. "If they didn't want me to do this, they should have told me a long time ago that it was so horrible." I really believed it too. But I decided not to push my luck. I could dismiss the far-off threat of the fires of hell, but my eyesight was a different matter. From that point on, my mother was always surprised and puzzled that despite my total lack of organization in all other areas of my life, I was a zealot in monitoring the frequency and outcome of my visits to the ophthalmologist.

✢ BETRAYAL

I WAS TEN when I first experienced real guilt. Until then, the judgment of my behavior existed outside of me: in a parent, a teacher, a neighbor. Even though I knew that certain behaviors like lying and stealing were wrong, I never felt very bad about them, unless I got caught. Then the bad feeling was one of shame and fear, not guilt.

The purpose of guilt in our lives is to make us feel so bad, wrong, anxious, unworthy, shitty, unlovable, and the absolute scum of the earth that we will never, ever want to feel that way again. So a healthy dose of guilt can strengthen our resolve to never sin. Not ever. Well, at least not until the next time the temptation arises, and we forget the pain of it all, just like childbirth, and jump right back into the action.

I learned this lesson in the winter of fifth grade. Right before the Christmas break, Richard Flynn intentionally broke the thermometer on what was optimistically called the "science table" (a Bunsen burner, a beaker, and a compass), the pride and joy of Sister Fatima. That offense, combined with the fact that this was his third year in fifth grade, got him promptly expelled. This finally allowed me to leave public school and take my place among the chosen at Our Lady Queen of Angels.

By the end of the first day, I didn't know the name of the principal, but I could name the three most popular girls in my grade. They clustered together in the school yard, linking pinkies as they skipped along the pavement at recess. They passed notes, and clearly had the attention of all the cute boys. Even though we all wore the exact same pleated green-plaid uniforms, with green kneesocks and brown oxfords, they looked almost stylish in theirs. I felt like a freak in mine, and in my vigilant, self-conscious, preadolescent mind, I was sure that everyone could automatically tell that it was a hand-me-down from my next-door neighbor.

That night, lying across my bed with a notebook in my hand, I looked like I was doing my homework. And in a way, I was. I was exploring the age-old sociological questions of how people enter into groups and, once in, how they develop and maintain their status. This was the beginning of a ten-year period in which the only legitimate purpose of school to me was as a backdrop for playing out my social life.

My targets were Ann Marie, Caroline, and Judy. After several weeks of watching them, I felt I knew them well. But they were so wrapped up in their little group that they wouldn't have recognized me if they had tripped over me in the girls' bathroom. I gave out every signal I knew that I was interested in being their friend. But there was an invisible wall around them that I could not penetrate.

Other girls invited me over after school and I refused, wanting to leave open the possibility that one of the cool girls would call. My mother was puzzled by my reticence at accepting invitations. She had the misinformed notion that as long as a person was "nice," she was "cool." I gave her the same look that my daughter gives me now when a new boy leaves our house and I say, "He seems like a nice boy." My daughter sneers at me with one of those what-rock-did-you-climb-out-from-under looks and I know I will not be laying eyes on that boy again.

There was a girl named Maureen Russell who had been nice to me from my first day of school. She let me look on with her in the books I hadn't gotten yet. She pointed out the relevant information about school that grown-ups never bother to tell you. Maureen had beautiful hair and a body that had clearly gotten a jump on the rest of us. But she still had a round baby face and had not yet adopted any affectations of being "cool." She invited me to her house after school. Unlike everyone I knew—all "walkers"—Maureen lived "on the other side of town," a concept I never really understood but vaguely felt wasn't good.

But her house looked great to me. It had thick lime-green shag carpeting and modern furniture. She had a white canopy bed with a pink bedspread, something I had longed for my entire life.

Maureen's mother won the award for the person who looked least like a mother of a ten-year-old. She looked more like a Barbie doll, with her hair all teased up and long fingernails with scream-ing red polish. In the middle of the day, she wore short shorts with backless gold spiked heels. I don't remember her ever with-out a cigarette dangling from her lips. She smoked in this really elegant way, as if she were emphasizing a point with each exhala-tion. She held the record for the person who could go the longest without flicking her cigarette ashes. Sometimes I'd get so entranced by her cigarette tip that I'd forget what she was saying. There was always Coke in the refrigerator and potato chips in the cupboard. In a showdown between Maureen and her mother, I would have chosen her mother, but I was growing to like Maureen too.

Over time, we became real friends. We listened to music and argued daily about who was better, Dr. Kildare (me) or Ben Casey (Maureen). We linked pinkies on the playground. I never forgot about the cool girls, and they never strayed from my peripheral vi-sion. But I wasn't alone anymore and that was what mattered.

Maureen encouraged me to join the choir, to which almost every girl belonged. Choir was fun. Sister Margaret Joseph was one of the best nuns, let alone women, that I had ever known. Because I was a second soprano, I was placed next to two of the cool girls, Ann Marie and Caroline. Maureen, being an alto, was a few rows back. As was my tendency in situations I enjoyed, I began to make smart-ass remarks that were, to my great pleasure, thoroughly en-joyed by Ann Marie and Caroline. After a week of acknowledging my existence, Ann Marie approached me at recess and asked if I wanted to go to the public library with them after school. Going to the Easton Public Library after a long day of school was not a thing that I thought cool people did, but I readily agreed. As an af-terthought, I asked if Maureen could come too. Ann Marie wrin-kled up her nose and sneered, "No!" as though she couldn't believe my effrontery.

Late in the school day, Maureen passed me a note, confirming the fact that I was still coming over to her house as we had arranged. I wrote back to her saying that I had remembered a dentist appointment and couldn't come. It was a lie. And unlike the lies I told to grown-ups or my brothers and sisters, which didn't count, I could feel this one register somewhere in the pit of my stomach and it didn't feel good. I tried to concentrate on the prized invitation, rather than the fabrication. Maureen wished me good luck at the dentist, and my eyes felt so heavy that it was difficult to meet hers. I waited until she drove off with her mother and then ran to join the girls.

The true reason for the trip to the library was scholastic only in the broadest sense. Judy's older sister, Teresa, had told her about an unbelievable book about "doing it" called *The Group* by Mary McCarthy. Her sister said that all the "good stuff" was in chapter 2. Caroline, who was by far the boldest of us all, went to the geography section and pulled down the biggest atlas she could find. Then she walked right over to the fiction section, scanned the M's, and plucked the book off the shelf, tucking it inside the atlas.

We gathered around her at the table farthest away from the librarian's desk.

And we started to read. Chapter 2 is a graphic, almost clinical, recounting of a woman's first time, and it was like dynamite in the hands of girls who had been given only the most cursory information about menstruation, which was presented to us as all we ever needed to know about sex. We were beside ourselves. Someone was constantly blushing, giggling, or exclaiming "Oh my God!" as we pored over the pages. I was thrilled to be gaining all this valuable information, but I was even happier that I was sharing this rite of passage with these girls. Jumping from total sexual ignorance to at least partial knowledge through our own guts and wits had a unifying we-all-have-a-secret feeling to it.

As we walked home, the girls began making plans for the next day. Someone had heard that *Peyton Place* was a pretty racy book, and God knows, we figured we needed to get as much knowledge as we could. I couldn't tell whether they were asking me to join them, so I kept my mouth shut. When Caroline asked if I could come, I almost sang out my assent. And then I remembered Maureen. I told them I had made plans to do something with her.

"Why do you hang around with her?" Judy demanded.

Watchful of my every word, I answered, "'Cause she's pretty nice."

"Well, she's a slut," pronounced Ann Marie in that age-old way that girls malign each other.

I was fairly sure that Maureen was equally as inexperienced and probably less knowledgeable than we were.

"How do you know she's a slut?" I ventured.

"Because my brother in the eighth grade said that she let Frankie McManus get to second base with her."

"I don't think she even knows Frankie McManus," I answered.

But then I had all three of them to contend with, "Well, you know about her mother, don't you?"

"What about her?" I asked.

"She *works*," sneered Judy.

"In a *diner*," added Caroline.

And Ann Marie, confident that she held the trump card, concluded, "And . . . she's *divorced!*"

I knew none of those things about Mrs. Russell. All three of them were definite variants in a homogeneous parish in which no one's mother worked, especially in a diner. And no one, no one was divorced.

I wanted to tell them how really cool Mrs. Russell was. But I knew that anything I said to make the Russells look better would make me look worse. I swallowed my words. I swallowed them so hard that they burned in my chest as I experienced, for the second time in two days, the sense that I was involved in something terribly wrong.

Over time, I spent more time with the cool girls and less time with Maureen. There was a silent agreement between Maureen and me that we did not talk about the other girls, as if she knew that if she asked, she would not like the answers.

Though I spent less time with Maureen, my new group was still not content. They set up blatant challenges to my loyalty in all those tiny cruelties that preadolescent girls become expert at inflicting upon one another. If I was talking with Maureen on the playground, one of them would run up to me laughing, tug at my sleeve, yell, "Come here. We've got to tell you something!" and drag me away. I would give Maureen an apologetic look that said "This is all out of my control" and would utter empty words like "I'll be right back." But I never was "right back." That was the point of the whole exercise.

As if to test my loyalty to them, they continually upped the ante, so that I constantly had to choose between Maureen and them. I always chose them, while trying to give Maureen just enough to deceive myself into thinking I was still being a good friend.

One Sunday when we were sitting in the choir loft, an all-out assault was launched. Judy, an alto like Maureen, whispered, "What's that smell?" She began sniffing around Maureen. Between hymns, when Sister Margaret Joseph wasn't looking, Caroline and Ann Marie turned around and said, "I don't know, but I think it's coming from there," and pointed to Maureen. Caroline poked me to join in. I was silent and kept my head down, pretending to read the text of "Kyrie Eleison," which was our next piece. In a stage whisper, Ann Marie leaned over her pew and hissed, "Martha, you better tell your friend that no amount of perfume is going to cover up the way she smells." Everyone around us was laughing. I kept my head down, still pretending to be engrossed in the hymnal. "Martha! . . . Martha! . . . " Judy demanded. Caroline and Ann Marie were nudging me on both sides—I had to turn around. When I did, I faced not only Judy, but Maureen, who was sitting right next to her. Maureen's face was white, and her eyes were liquid with tears and pain. "Tell her, Martha . . ." chanted the girls in unison. "Tell *them*, Martha . . ." pleaded Maureen in silence. I looked at Judy and I looked at Maureen. And then I turned around. I looked back down and hid within my hymnal. Mercifully, the acolyte rang the bells on the altar and we all sang in perfect synchrony after the priest:

> Kyrie eleison (Lord have mercy)
> Christe eleison (Christ have mercy)
> Kyrie eleison (Lord have mercy)

I kept my face bent low in the book through the entire mass. I mouthed the words, afraid of any sound that might come from my mouth.

I tried to reassure myself with the technically correct but flimsy excuse that I had been silent because one was not supposed to talk in church. But I knew that by doing nothing, I had done something very wrong. It didn't fit into the catalog of sins I had memorized so well, and certainly didn't feel like anything that a priest could wipe away with a few Hail Marys. I remembered the story of Peter, who denied even knowing his best friend Jesus. Not just once, but three times. At the time when Jesus needed him most, Peter took a hike. For years I had pictured Peter as such a wimp, to deny his connection to Jesus. But now, in my identification with Peter, I reasoned that he probably had a good reason for denying that he knew Christ. He could have gotten himself killed, and how would that have changed anything for Jesus anyway?

It would have been nice if that rationalization had helped me, but it didn't. I knew that even though I sat reverent and straight-backed in that church pew, all the while I was really dancing with the devil. I was saying, "Give me these girls as friends. I won't be cruel. But neither will I be kind. Is that really so bad?"

The joy of belonging was tempered by the guilt of rejecting. It was the first time in my life that I had ever felt truly responsible for my behavior. I was appalled at myself for letting my friend be crucified in that church. No, I never actually used the hammer, but I stood by and held the nails. And that was just as bad. It was then I knew that often the greatest of sins are not the things we do but the things we fail to do. This revelation confused the hell out of me then and continues to plague me now.

Lost in the dark forest without a moral compass, I longed for the times when someone else would judge my behavior, forgive me for it, and provide me with a clear formula for suddenly and magically making everything all better.

❧ MADONNA AND MEDUSA

HAVING A CHILD brought out the best in me. It also brought out the worst.

After years in which I dismissed evil and sin as not even slightly relevant to my life, motherhood made me confront my own darkness. I had always known that it was there. I knew it in the rage I often felt at having to divide more and more limited turf with each new sibling. I knew it in the wrestling-to-the-ground, I'll-rip-your-face-off fights I had with my brother, in which I was sure one or both of us were going to end up dead. I knew it in the panic I felt as my mother's resources dramatically decreased as the size of our family increased. I knew it in the fury that, as the oldest girl, I was the assistant mother to children I both loved and resented.

One night my mother asked me to put one child to bed while she bathed two others, all of them in various stages of combative exhaustion and disintegration. I was watching *The Patty Duke Show*, which I dearly loved. I tried to put her off until the end of the show, but she demanded that I come immediately. I stomped up the stairs, burst into the bathroom, and screamed out, "Why do we have to have so many kids in this family?" With a soapy hand, my mother brushed away a piece of hair from her forehead and in a deceptively even, level voice said, "And exactly whom would you get rid of, Martha?" I felt absolutely and completely ashamed. And I knew right then that there was only one place to go with that kind of anger—underground, where no one could get hurt.

As my life came more under my own control, those ugly, shameful feelings of hate and rage seemed to diminish to the point of vanishing. What I didn't know was that all those feelings were still in my account and that by the time I had my own child, they had collected a lot of interest.

Just as no one had prepared me for how truly awful childbirth was, no one could possibly have found the language to communicate the rapture of producing a new life. Loving a man is one kind of love. Loving a child is another. Although I always said that I would jump in front of a speeding train to spare my husband, I was never totally sure, should the situation arise, that I would actually do it. But from the moment I held that sweet child in my arms, I knew that not only would I jump in front of a speeding train, I would leap tall buildings in a single bound for my baby.

After staying at home with a screaming, sleepless, colicky baby, I realized another crucial fact of motherhood. In a matter of two days, I went from Madonna to Medusa. I should have known from my marriage how you can madly love someone and maniacally hate him at the same time. But my husband was my equal, my partner. Keara was my child. My sweet, innocent child whom I wanted to throw against the wall. In the face of seven pounds of unremitting, inconsolable screaming, I had never known such endless powerlessness in my life. Nothing I tried worked. I was chronically and seriously sleep-deprived, leaking from just about every orifice possible, and sure that a serious mistake had been made in the hospital and I had been given Satan's baby, or at the very least, the child of a crack user. People told me how children change your life. They told me that childbirth was basically a bitch. They gave me tips about toughening my nipples and pumping my breasts. But no one ever told me that you could hate your kid. I didn't know whether they didn't talk about it because it only happens to ruthless child abusers, or because it happens to everyone and they're just too ashamed to admit it.

In my training as a psychologist, I had been constantly appalled by the people who abused their children. Some of them were sadistic sons of bitches who also chronically beat their wives and were now just diversifying their targets of cruelty. But others were young, overwhelmed mothers who just "lost it." And unlike me, they had no backups, no time-outs, no one to say, "I know what you're feeling, honey. We've all been there." But before my own baby, those young mothers certainly didn't get much empathy from me. They got suggestions, advice, and training in "self-control strategies." What they could have gotten was, "It must be so scary to lose control like that with your baby." But instead, they got warnings and a report to the Department of Social Services. All the things I did were correct, but they weren't enough. Real life gives you an empathy for darkness that you can't get in any school. And the more you know your own darkness, the better you can relate to someone else's. Not accept it. Not condone it. But relate to it.

At the sacraments of marriage, in which two people are joined together, and baptism, in which a child is joined to a family and welcomed into the church, the rituals are typically concluded by the lighting of a candle, given to the participants as a symbol of the light of Christ. It is a beautiful moment and one that often leaves me clearing my throat and wiping my eyes. But I've begun to think that maybe, along with a candle, the presider should present the couple or the family with a gun (unloaded, of course) to symbolize the fact that sometimes the greatest amount of pain, the strongest expressions of hate, the most frequent expressions

Martha Manning

of violence, and the most comfortable home for sin live within these families we are blessing.

The Thanksgiving when Keara was five, she and I were in the laundry room, standing in a pile of clothes that had not been folded in weeks. I kept rifling around for something for her to wear to my parents' house for dinner. She refused each outfit I retrieved from the pile, haughtily giving her reasons for the rejections. I finally held up one dress and said, "You are going to wear this," to which she responded, "No, I am not!" We went back and forth with this exchange several times. Then she folded her arms, stuck out her chin, and said, "And you can't make me!" What happened inside me was like the snapping of a rubber band that has been pulled and held under great pressure for too long.

I slapped her across the face. We both stood there, stunned. She screwed up her mouth, tightened her stance, and clearly continued to refuse to wear the dress. I was as angry as I have ever been in my life. She wasn't even giving me the satisfaction of crying the tears that were so clearly trapped in me. I slapped her again, so hard that her hand flew to her face. Her cheek was red and I could see the white outline of the prints of my fingers. She burst into sobbing, wracking tears. She ran up the stairs and into her room. I sat down in the mountain of laundry, some of it clean, some of it filthy, and cried until my head ached, until there was crying in my throat but no more fluid for tears.

I approached her room tentatively and could hear her crying on the bed. I hugged her and cried, "Keara, I'm sorry. I'm so sorry. I should never have done that. Never." And Keara cried back, "I was bad, I was really bad. You never would have done that if I didn't deserve it." I pulled myself together enough to tell her that she was absolutely wrong. That I lost control and that no child deserves to get slapped across her face by her mother—for anything. By then the red-and-white imprint of my hand had disappeared, but the fissure that it caused in our rock-solid relationship remained.

Chasing Grace

There was an uneasy silence between us for the whole day. At dinner, my mother noted that Keara was not her usually ebullient self and wondered why.

I said that I didn't know.

I can still feel the reverberation of that slap between Keara and me. That moment when I stopped relating to her as my child and treated her as an object that could absorb my own frustration and distress. She remembers it, too. Once or twice a year, usually in front of other people, she will say, "I *still* remember when you slapped me . . . *for no good reason.*" She takes quiet and righteous pleasure in the fact that I still squirm, even after twelve years. Whenever the subject arises, her final words are always the same, "And Mom, if you ever do that again, I'll slap you right back." And all I can say is, "Okay."

❧ BEING BAD ON THE PLANE

SEVERAL MONTHS AGO, my flight from Washington to Boston was delayed for an hour on the ground, leaving many of us with the knowledge that when the plane finally did take off, we'd barely make our connecting flights, or miss them entirely. Boston was to be the final destination for only about three people on the plane. The rest of us were upset. Throughout the flight, the call button rang constantly. Each distressed passenger seemed compelled to share his or her misfortune with the flight attendants, who couldn't do a damn thing about it but listened anyway. They took notes and assured the passengers that an airline representative would meet them at the gate, which really meant that someone would show up to tell them what they already knew— they'd missed their flights and this might be the perfect time to get to know Logan airport.

The length of our delay in such close quarters broke through the typical reserve on an airplane, where the decorum demands that passengers remain within their own space, occupied with laptops or books, feigning or really sleeping, looking out the window, or engaging in any other activity that requires as little eye contact, touching, and verbal interaction as possible. At least, that's what I always expect the decorum should be. In reality, I suspect that right before he drops me off, my husband tapes a piece of paper to my back that says, "Please, talk to me. I'm lonely. Distract me from my misery by telling me yours . . . for the entire trip."

As it became clear during the flight that we were not making up the time we'd spent on the ground, people began commiserating with one another about who was the worst off. I had a wedding to attend in Maine, and was booked on a tiny bus with wings. If I missed it, it would be hours before I'd get another. But the internationally screwed had little sympathy with those of us who were merely East Coast–screwed.

As the plane touched down in Boston and began taxiing the runway, the rustling around for purses and bags began with some urgency. With a reminder from Kelly, the flight attendant, that we had to wait until the plane came to a complete stop at the gate, we reluctantly sat down. One really irritated-looking guy leapt up, yanked his suitcase from the overhead compartment, and sprinted down the aisle. The man had more gold around his neck than my mother has in her entire jewelry box. He was tan and hairy—one of those guys you can tell is obnoxious from a hundred yards away. His defiance of the rules commanded everyone's attention. When he reached the first row of "no class" (as opposed to first-class) seats, Staci, another flight attendant, blocked his passage. Staci is the kind of young woman I can't let myself look at for too long, because I will end up feeling very bad. She probably weighed no more than 105 pounds, had perfect teeth, gorgeous hair, and a perky personality. But as the guy approached first class, her don't-mess-with-me look made her a force to be reckoned with.

Staci demanded that the tan hairy man sit down. He refused. People stopped fiddling with their luggage. This was starting to look interesting. Kelly came to Staci's aid and told the man again to sit down. Again, he refused. Then Todd, the first-class flight attendant, joined the fray. As a passenger, I felt tremendous ambivalence about what I was witnessing. I knew it was important to obey orders on an airplane, but on some level I also wanted to do what that guy was doing. I wanted to yell, "Screw you guys; *you and your stupid airline* made me late. To hell with your lousy rules!" and dash to make my next flight. I had the sense that I wasn't the only one on the fence about this. But it was clear we weren't a group organized for mutiny.

This absolute defiance of authority was riveting. It had been a long time since I'd been in a group where we had been told to do something by someone "in charge" and one person directly refused to comply. The situation was a standoff. As the man and the flight attendants argued, we passengers began to look at each other and make faces. Then people started talking out loud, at first to each other ("I wish he'd just sit down"), and then to him ("Hey, buddy, siddown, willya?"). The passenger consensus had no impact on him.

Finally, Staci put her hands on her hips and threatened that if he didn't go back to his seat immediately, she was going to TELL THE CAPTAIN! Anyone who wasn't already monitoring the action started to then. Staci knocked on the pilot's door and closed it behind her. Several seconds later, she emerged triumphant. The plane came to a sudden and complete halt, still quite a distance from the gate. The captain came over the loudspeaker vowing, "I will not move this plane until everyone, and I mean *everyone*, is seated." The guy didn't move.

My face was hot. I began to sweat. My skin felt too tight. There were fish swimming around in my stomach. I knew this situation. And I knew the feeling. It was guilt. Other passengers were angry, frustrated, upset, and anxious. But I felt guilty. Embedded since childhood, this particular brand of guilt has been covered over by many years but can still be easily activated under the right conditions.

Martha Manning

🌺 NO ONE IS GETTING OUT OF HERE . . .

IN GRADE SCHOOL, whenever someone broke a rule, Sister Perpetua laid down the law: "No one is leaving this room until the person who did this . . ."—took the milk money, talked while she was out of the room, pushed the class saint on the playground, looked at the dirty magazine discovered in the boys' bathroom—confessed, *or* was turned in.

At these moments, regardless of my innocence, all I could feel was guilt. It burned my ears, churned in the pit of my stomach, and curled my toes tight. I felt guilty because I wished I *had* stolen the milk money. I *would* have been talking if I hadn't been in the bathroom when Sister was out of the room. I *had* wanted to smack Miss Perfect Louise Rafferty for over a year and was pleased when someone else finally did it. And I would even have looked at the dirty magazine. I would have done all these things. The fact that I didn't owed more to a lack of guts than to any moral character on my part. In the Catholic church, if you even "entertained" (invited it to come in and stay for a while) a wicked or lustful thought, you had already sinned. Thinking it was as bad as doing it.

Sitting erect, hands folded on our desks, in stone silence as the big black-rimmed clock ticked out the vastness of time between 2:00 and our 3:00 dismissal bordered on the impossible. But when we were still sitting there after the final bell at 3:01, we knew we were in for the long haul. It was Sister Perpetua's promise, and my belief, that she would keep us there for as long as she wanted. Through the afternoon, overnight, through the week. Until the guilty party confessed or was identified.

I never thought the whole thing out rationally, as I would in later years. ("Yeah, like she's really gonna call fifty sets of parents.") At the age of ten, I still thought a form of instant telepathy existed between parents, teachers, and church. Our parents entrusted us to the nuns during the day, no questions asked. A complaint that Sister smacked your hand with a ruler was not usually met with sympathy in most households. The very fact that you were punished was considered *proof* of your misbehavior, and if you weren't careful, you could get yourself in more trouble—punished two times for the same crime. There was no telling how far the nuns would go with their threats. It's not like they had a lot going on at home. These women could afford to follow through.

All of us had been involved in standoffs before. They usually involved a difference of opinion between parent and child about the amount and type of food that had to be consumed as a prerequisite for leaving the table. The standoffs at home typically involved a test of wills between two people. The rest of the family did not have to suffer and were allowed to go about their business while the picky eater watched his food cool and night fall.

But classroom standoffs involved everyone. One person's sins became everyone's burden. You were expected to turn yourself in, as well as everyone else you observed misbehaving. All of these expectations occurred in an environment where adults demonstrated a total lack of trust in us. It was an honor system without the honor.

So I sat there with my red-hot face, hands and toes curled like claws, and meditated on the clock as it moved past dismissal time and I wondered how long it would be before someone cracked the code of silence that defined our unlikely kinship. If no one cracked within the first five minutes of "staying after," it was likely that no one would. So, after about twenty horrible minutes of Sister Perpetua pacing the aisles, staring people down, and punishing us with her awful silence, it was always *she* who cracked. She'd sputter something like, "Get out of here, the lot of you. I can't stand the sight of you." As we scrambled out of our seats and hustled for the door before she changed her mind, she tried to recover her authority by yelling, "Don't think we're finished with this. I won't forget it."

Martha Manning

She was truly disgusted with all of us—even her favorites. Despite the fact that only a few of the fifty children were the actual perpetrators, she expected loyalty from everyone else. Once she put out an all-points bulletin and found that we refused to cooperate with the manhunt, we were all *equally* bad in her eyes.

✿ LOST

CATHOLIC CHILDREN are used to guilt by association. Hell, we were guilty before the ink dried on our birth certificates. According to the tenets of our faith, we were all born with original sin. No tabula rasa for us. We started off at a handicap. Born *looking* beautiful and innocent, we were tainted in the same invisible way that bad genes are transmitted from one generation to the next. As sin goes, it was hardly original. It is more like revisited sin, regurgitated sin, generational sin. With baptism, we were freed from original sin. But it didn't take with me. I am still one of the guiltiest people I know. Not the baddest, just the guiltiest.

There are no absolutes about guilt. For some people, a little goes a long, long way. And for others, a lot goes nowhere. Guilt is a sophisticated experience. It involves being able to feel bad about a transgression, regardless of its outcome. If our parents and teachers train us right, we associate doing bad things with a loss of their approval and love. The ability to do this is usually a product of the I'm-so-disappointed-in-you school of behavior management. If they do it with enough frequency and finesse, after a while we don't need our parents in sight to feel those lousy feelings. We begin to take over all roles: the accused, the judge, and the jury. We can make ourselves feel like pond scum without ever having to go anywhere or talk to anyone. The action is totally internal.

The major function of guilt is not so much to make us feel bad *after* we've sinned, but to build in an alarm system that sounds every time we even begin to venture into badness.

I stand in the dime store and survey the merchandise with lust. *God, I'd love to have that lipstick and it's so close and I have no money and the cashiers at Woolworth's are always mean anyway, plus it's not like it comes out of their paychecks . . .* But then comes the feeling in the pit of my stomach, the fluttering in my chest. My heart beats fast. I start to sweat. Words pop into my head like *low-life idiot* and *stupid asshole.* All of a sudden, I have relentless visions of my mother crying, my family reduced to paupers, and any number of natural disasters.

And the beauty of it is that it has nothing to do with being nailed for my crime. Nothing. Woolworth's could be totally empty. The blusher could have fallen off the shelf and into my pocket. It makes no difference. The matter is now a closed circuit, between me, myself, and I. It's the id, the ego, and the superego. I am giving myself a preview, serving up an appetizer, a bit of bile on toast—enough to give me a taste for the four-course torment of a meal that I will suffer if I commit the crime.

My parents and my teachers did a wonderful job. I have a superego so powerful it could get Los Angeles under control. My parents were incredibly adept at the we're-so-disappointed-in-you method of guilt induction. It was a powerful technique because, unlike the sting of punishment, which disappeared whenever the sentence was up, guilt had no clear ending. There was no one day when all of a sudden my parents said, "All right, time's up. We're not disappointed in you anymore."

It was a lot like being lost, a condition equally distressing to me. One evening when we were returning from visiting an old friend in the city, my mother was studying the map as she drove. Tiring of four of us kids engaged in brutal voice-to-voice and hand-to-hand combat, she yelled back, "Be quiet, we're lost." It scared us still and silent. My mother, who always seemed to know where she was going, suddenly didn't have a clue. *Lost* was not a relative word to me. It was a frightening concept, because it was linked in my mind with *forever.* We stayed quiet for the entire ride. I prayed alternately to Saint Christopher, patron saint of travelers, and Saint Jude, patron saint of lost causes—just to cover all the bases. My prayers never involved simple begging. I felt I had a much better shot if I made a deal right up front. "Saint Christopher, if you get us home, I promise to be nice to my brother for one whole day." "Saint Jude, if you help my mother, I'll say the rosary every day for a week."

After an hour, things started to look familiar. Finally, we were on our street, with our gray split-level in sight, thanking God and anyone else whose powers we had invoked during that quiet, scary ride. The fact that telling us we were lost worked like a cattle prod was not wasted on my mother. In desperate situations, she would pull it out again, when she knew perfectly well where she was going but wasn't sure she'd get there without killing at least one of us first. So every now and then, she told us she was lost. It always worked. I became instantly anxious, shut up, and behaved myself for the rest of the ride. The problem with telling us we were lost was that she never told us when we were "found." We'd drive for long periods in a state of heightened anxiety, fearing that Long Island might have its own Bermuda Triangle where suburban mothers and children in wood-paneled station wagons dropped out of sight for all eternity. Guilt is a lot like that.

Another technique that I can only admire in retrospect involved requiring us to choose our own punishment for the really big infractions. When I was fifteen, I was arrested for shoplifting a record by the Four Tops, "Reach Out" (a direct invitation if ever there was one). My parents told me how disappointed they were in me, how I had threatened my father's standing in the FBI because he was supposed to report my brush with the law to J. Edgar Hoover, which meant we would probably be packing for Butte, Montana, in the near future. I let my parents know that I felt lower than mold. Then they told me to choose my punishment. This was always a difficult one because I didn't want to give myself something that was so easy they would think I was blowing off the situation. But I also didn't want to assign anything harder than they themselves would dish out. The only big thing I had planned was my first "Beach Week" (chaperoned by someone's older sister) when school got out a month later. Judging from my mother's tears, which were infrequent, and my father's quiet, I chose grounding for Beach Week as the appropriate punishment. After a consultation behind closed doors, my parents concurred. I still wonder whether I overshot that one. And I'll never know, because they still refuse to tell me.

Another brilliant aspect of guilt induction was the way my mother handled the inevitability that with so many children, she would regularly nail the wrong person for a crime. Once unjustly accused, I would voice vigorous, righteously outraged-and-innocent protestations that I didn't hit my sister, get into my mother's makeup, or mess up the playroom, always with the phrase, "But it's not fair!" My mother's calm response to my lament was, "Well, just apply it to something you did do wrong and didn't get caught for." It was then I learned that there are no statutes of limitation on guilt.

And maybe there shouldn't be. Guilt is not an altogether bad thing. It involves thinking before you act, imagining the outcomes of what you do—on yourself and on other people. It involves stopping yourself from running a red light or blowing someone's face off, even when the chances of getting caught are nil. The significant emphasis on neuroses and guilt in the psychology and psychiatry of the past four decades has undermined the need to take responsibility for one's actions. People aren't bad anymore; they're sick, meaning they can't be held fully culpable. Sometimes they *are* sick. They have serious bona fide mental illnesses that compromise their judgment and responsibility. But there are many people who deserve only the diagnoses "just plain rotten."

I am frightened about where we're headed as we become less guilty and responsible for our actions. So far, things don't look good. We cringe at the concept of sin, and yet the evil in the world is so overwhelming that we cannot divest ourselves of culpability. We *have* sinned. We *should* feel guilty about the disparity of wealth in the world. We *should* feel guilty about the rampant neglect and abuse of children. We *should* feel guilty about the violence that characterizes our culture. I see the danger of this guilt-free, irresponsible world for my own child, and I am terrified of letting her go. Now *I* want to scream out, *We're lost,* and keep screaming it until I'm absolutely sure that we're found.

❧ HOLOCAUST

ONE MORNING last year, I began the day as haphazardly as most others. The clock by my bed read 7:35. I had an 8:00 patient. Another late night, poor planning, and an indifferent alarm clock sent me scrambling for clothes, breakfast, briefcases, and cash. I dashed out the door with wet hair, no makeup, and my daughter yelling to me that I was wearing one black knee-high stocking and one blue one. I was too late to care. I checked my watch to begin the countdown. On my best day I can make it to the office in twelve minutes and thirty seconds. I had exactly fifteen minutes until my first appointment. No problem.

But I wasn't prepared for the two lanes in my direction to be reduced to one because of road repairs. At the first cross street, a late-model green Mercedes pulled out in front of me as slowly and cautiously as a big rig negotiating a hairpin turn. I knew then that I was in trouble. But I decided that the road repairs would end shortly and I would buzz past the Mercedes immediately.

At the stoplight, I checked my appointment book: two patients, a lecture to my first-year doctoral students, and then two free hours to use my long-awaited ticket to tour the newly opened Holocaust Memorial Museum. It was critical that I remain on schedule.

The women in the Mercedes ahead of me looked and drove exactly like my grandmother when she was in her eighties. Their pleasant conversation seemed to take priority over the efficient operation of a motor vehicle. The driver kept her foot on the brake, keeping us crawling at twenty miles per hour rather than the posted forty. She came to a dead stop in the middle of the road to allow pedestrians to jaywalk. She stopped several hundred yards before yellow lights. At stop signs, despite no cross traffic, she looked like she was waiting for a personal invitation to continue her journey.

I began to really dislike this woman. At first it was her ostentatious green Mercedes, then it was her I LOVE ANIMALS . . . THEY'RE DELICIOUS bumper sticker pasted right next to one that pictured a fetus and said RESPECT LIFE. As my dashboard clock told me there was no way, short of my car sprouting wings, that I was going to get to my office on time, I got angrier and angrier, slamming my hand against the steering wheel and uttering foul language in all possible combinations and permutations. I remembered a recent movie star who, in his own particular brand of roadside justice, applied a golf club to a car that had wronged him. I found myself wondering if I had any similar blunt objects in my trunk. I wanted to make a citizen's arrest, issuing her a warrant for impeding the healthy flow of traffic and for frustrating people who had more important things to do than take in the sights and gossip with friends.

Finally, the road repairs ended. I gunned the engine like some adolescent punk and entered the other lane. I came up next to her at the stoplight. In my fury, I glowered at her and shook my fist. She squinted at me as if she were trying to recognize me and then smiled broadly and even waved at me. I shook my fist again. Her friend leaned over and waved to me, too. Over the sound of traffic, I yelled, "You drive like shit." She just smiled and turned back to her friend.

They wouldn't even give me the satisfaction of an angry, unpleasant interaction, in which I could then blame them for at least some of the ugliness of the experience. I HATED THEM.

I arrived ten minutes late at my office. My first patient immediately noted that my stockings didn't match, and it was downhill from there. The next two hours were spent attempting to put aside my own rage so that I could help other people with theirs.

I was late for my lecture. I was late for my scheduled tour of the Holocaust museum. But I parked illegally and talked my way in, despite my tardiness.

The United States Holocaust Memorial Museum, in Washington, D.C., is dedicated to "presenting the history of the persecution and murder of 6 million Jews and millions of other victims of Nazi tyranny from 1933 to 1945." The introductory brochure notes that the museum's "primary mission is to inform Americans about this unprecedented tragedy, to remember those who suffered, and to inspire visitors to contemplate the moral implications of their choices and responsibilities as citizens in an interdependent world."

Upon entering the daunting four-story building, I exchanged my ticket for an identification card bearing the picture of a young girl named Berta Rivkina, a survivor, whose personal story I would be following through the exhibit. Being handed a name and a face provides a very different perspective from which to view an "exhibit." I immediately found myself "losing distance," feeling drawn not only into the horrific experience of this staggering number of people, but into the experience of this one young woman who lived in a ghetto and very narrowly escaped execution several times. It was strange. I kept finding myself unconsciously trying to stuff her card deep in my pocket, knowing somehow that it was easier to absorb this horror in its totality than in the story of one young girl the exact same age as my daughter.

The museum contains thousands of photos and documents—exacting accounts of such unimaginable brutality as the slaughter at Babi Yar, where, as the poet Yevgeny Yevtushenko said, "all things scream silently." More than thirty-three thousand Jews were systematically killed there in only two days.

I felt myself becoming almost numb staring at the documentation. How do I process such information? What does the mind do with it? One thing I do in situations like these is to distance myself from the victims. I say things like, "It was a long time ago" and "They were different times, different cultures." Another thing I do is to distance myself from the perpetrators. "They are animals, anomalies in a culture that would never allow them to do that now." Then it all falls into place. I can feel pity for the victims (the Jews) and disgust for the perpetrators (the Nazis). The beauty of it is that I never have to enter this particular equation at all.

It was easier for me to walk quickly past the photos than some of the other displays. The most penetrating exhibits were the ones that spoke not to the differences between *them* and *me* but to the similarities: pictures of large, happy families, their genealogies, their houses, their schools, their stories.

But nothing got to me like the shoes. Behind a huge plate of glass was a display of thousands of shoes confiscated from people who were later slaughtered. A sexy red sling-back high heel lay atop a sturdy black work boot. A tan leather sandal rested against a little girl's shiny Mary Jane. And wedged in the middle of a pile sat a tiny white baby shoe, just like the ones that sit bronzed on mantles. In that mountain was every kind and color of shoe that could be imagined. People walked this earth in them. They pulled them on each day with as little care or concern as we do now, never knowing that one day they would be ripped from them as a prelude to their deaths. Next to the display of shoes was a poem by Moses Shulstein: "We are the shoes. We are the last witnesses.

We are shoes from grandchildren and grandfathers from Prague, Paris and Amsterdam. And because we are only made of fabric and leather, and not of blood and flesh, each one of us avoided the hellfire."

Just when I felt that I had seen all I could bear, the corridor opened into a huge hall with a ceiling of light called the Hall of Remembrance. Hundreds of tiny flickering candles lined the walls. If the place could talk it would say, "Bear witness to all you have seen, but do not lose hope." It was a place that called for meditation, for prayer. But words eluded me. I wanted to lay prostrate on the ground under the generous slant of sunlight blessing the center of the room. I wanted to beg forgiveness for the "sins of my fathers."

But as I sat still in that room of light and silence, I felt called to do something else. I realized, as I leaned my elbows on my knees with my hands covering my face, that the Holocaust is not over. It is fluid, not fixed. It lives on in the streets of Sarajevo and Jerusalem, along the roads of Rwanda, in the horrors of Haiti. It is in Northern Ireland and Somalia. It is in my own neighborhood, where yesterday a junior-high-school boy was shot and killed by a companion of the same age.

But most frighteningly, I realized that there was something about being encased in tons of steel and glass that contributed to a total sense of separateness from the women in the Mercedes earlier that day. I was protected in my rage by a certain anonymity. She was a driver, a really bad driver—not a person. She was a frustration, a blockade to be overcome, a scapegoat for my frustration with my disorganized life.

Had there been a confessional box in the Hall of Remembrance, I would have availed myself of the sacrament of penance for the first time in twenty years. I would have pulled back the curtain, knelt on the cushion, and said, "Bless me, for I have sinned.

Bless me, for I am sinning now, and I usually don't even know it. Help me to remember how easily the Holocaust can live on in me, in the daily denial of the presence of God in others."

And I imagine the priest blessing me, knowing that any feeble attempts I make to live out that prayer will be the best act of contrition that a poor soul can make.

❧ ABSOLUTION

ASIDE FROM WORKING in soup kitchens and handing out food in parking lots, I have never had much contact with the actual people I was trying to help. There was always a middle-man—someone who took my money and did something good with it. In my more direct experiences with people in need, I was often "rewarded" by feeling like a combination of Dorothy Day and Lady Bountiful. But after I finished every shift, I went home. El Salvador was the first place I'd been where I didn't go home after a brief shift.

Catholic Relief Services invited me to El Salvador to survey their many creative projects aimed at keeping a fragile peace alive and rebuilding a war-torn country. I was there for two weeks. I was especially interested in the programs that targeted women— with such things as small business loans and training in herbal medicine and health care. In those two weeks I learned a great deal about El Salvador. But in some ways, I learned more about the United States government, of which I am a part. And most painfully, I learned about myself.

No one actually believed that I would make the trip. Despite the fact that I knew not a word of Spanish, or had any sense of what I was getting myself into, I said yes.

In my crash course on El Salvador before my departure, I learned a bit about this tiny country that has borne such a tremendous burden with such limited resources. I became aware that most

Salvadorans live in wretched poverty and have suffered for years in conditions in which their most basic human rights have been viciously abused. I knew most, of course, about the savage rapes and murders of the four American Catholic women, whose only sin was their attempt to upgrade the quality of people's lives. I knew about the six Jesuit priests and two women executed at a rectory. And I knew about the government-sanctioned murder of Archbishop Oscar Romero, who served as a beacon of light in the Salvadorans' struggle for justice.

In the month before I left for El Salvador, I read in horrifying detail in a *New Yorker* feature article about the systematic annihilation of the village of El Mozote, in which five hundred people were murdered by hanging, machete, burning, and shooting with American M–16 rifles and ammunition manufactured by the U.S. government in Lake City, Missouri. Many of the killers were trained by our own military. Of the five hundred killed, it is estimated that 90 percent were under the age of thirteen. For eleven years our government denied the massacre at El Mozote, discrediting all those who tried to speak the truth. It wasn't until a full excavation and evaluations of the remains of those slaughtered that our government acknowledged it as an atrocity. I wondered how a country that had known this much devastation could ever reconstruct itself into the "new El Salvador" that was promised.

The airport in San Salvador was like nothing I had ever seen, crammed to the rafters with people. I wasn't able to walk a foot without someone, usually a young child, begging for money. In my trip to the hotel, I was struck with the "Americanization" of the place—McDonald's, Burger King, Goodrich tires. Our guide pointed out the fences and the heavily armed guards around the houses of the rich people. There was no need to point out the poor people. They were everywhere. They clogged the streets selling from small stands. Industrious children darted between the wild traffic of San Salvador, begging from people in cars. Our driver told us that often children turn off the traffic lights and stand in the middle of these wild streets directing traffic, hoping to get tips. Others do "tricks" such as inhaling gasoline fumes, lighting them, and making it look like they are breathing fire.

As an American walking the streets of San Salvador, I was stopped constantly by people wearing T-shirts that said things like BALTIMORE ORIOLES and GUNS N' ROSES. They wanted me to know that they knew someone in "the States." Often they would point proudly to a T-shirt and say, "Virginia," "Texas," "New York."

In the middle of managing my way through the crowded streets, I was stung by a memory of something I had overheard several weeks before. I was at a party where the people were so rich that their flowered toilet paper matched the flowered wall-paper in the bathroom. Three women were talking about recent winter vacations in "the islands." One woman said, "Well, I'll never go *there* again. The beaches are beautiful, but there are so many poor people there. They're all over you. I just couldn't relax." I wanted to knock her into the lighted swimming pool at that time, but I had to admit to myself on those crowded streets where people pulled at me and my clothes, where they said loud things in Spanish that I didn't understand, where they begged and begged and begged, that there was a bit of that woman in me. I felt suffocated on those streets. And I felt every inch an "Anglo."

Most of my trip involved long rides in Land Rovers over rugged land that could only be called "roads" in the most nominal sense. This was where most of the war was fought, where most of the people suffered, and where the work of rebuilding and reconcilia-tion had to be most aggressive. While I was there to "see the sights," I knew that my main interest was in the stories of the people. Over the course of the two weeks, I got what I wanted. I heard the stories of the Salvadoran people. I also heard the stories of *my* people. I heard about the faith that the Salvadorans had put in "the States." They expressed their continuing confusion that our government sided with the small, rich, ruthless military over the people struggling to create a democracy like ours.

People ushered me into tin-roof huts with dirt floors and offered me corn tortillas baked over an open fire. They recounted stories of sons picked up by the military, never to be seen again. They showed pictures of families, pointing out the minority who were still alive. They told me of the incredible variety of ways that they had survived this long, horrible ordeal.

At first I was the writer, with the goal of gaining and recording information. I wrote furiously as my translator gave meaning to the heartfelt words coming from the women, men, and children who spoke with me. As the days went by, however, I began to realize that as these people recounted their horrors, they were not just talking about a foreign civil war in which the military was pitted against the rebels. They were talking about *my* country. The more they talked, the more I realized that I wasn't just a listener in this story: I was a player. I began to take fewer notes so that I could absorb their experience rather than just transcribe it.

When I learned about the Holocaust, I could arrogantly reassure myself that were it to happen today, the people of my generation would not allow it. But the people of my generation not only allowed the destruction of El Salvador, we *helped* it along. We didn't learn much from the Holocaust, because similar atrocities were still happening, often assisted or, at the very least, ignored by our government.

As the Salvadoran people told me about their loss and suffering, their experience came into sharper and sharper focus. I was reminded of my recent upgrade in contact lenses. At first I was delighted by the new acuity. But slowly I began to see things as they really were—the layers of dust carpeting my house, the small wrinkles around my eyes and mouth. I longed for the diffuse comfort of my weaker lenses and felt the burden of corrected vision.

With their stories of bravery, ingenuity, hardship, and suffering, the Salvadoran people strengthened my acuity. But with the acuity of their experience came a growing sorrow.

One afternoon I sat in a plaza against a hillside and spoke with a community organizer named Rosa. It was a gorgeous sunny day and people from the village were slowly trekking up the long hill to the place where mass would be said later that afternoon. Like many others, Rosa had fled from El Salvador over the border to Honduras. The refugees walked only at night, often taking as many as eight days to get to Honduras. They left with the clothes on their backs, thinking that they would be able to return to El Salvador in two or three months at most. However, they remained in Honduran refugee camps for nine years—crowded camps with few resources and no organization.

Rosa became an organizer in her camp, focusing on such basic needs as water, food, and the making of cooking utensils. While she had never seen herself as a leader before, she found that the conditions of the camp pushed her to new behaviors, new ways of being. She told me, "When you're afraid, you don't say what you have to say, but when you have to speak up for *others,* you have to overcome your fear and take responsibility." In the overcrowded camps, Rosa said, she had to "see the problems of others as mine."

I was frustrated in knowing that Rosa and I had more to talk about but that she was being careful with her words, as if she had given this explanation before and was suspicious of any type of journalist because of continued and justified distrust of the military. We dismissed the men as politely as possible. Then Rosa, our translator, and I sat together in the hot sun drinking warm beers. I asked her about her family. She had a nine-year-old and a seven-year-old. I asked about her husband. Her eyes filled, and I knew what she was telling me before the translator opened her mouth. After several years in the camp, Rosa was told by some new refugees that her husband, an FMLN guerrilla fighter, had been killed. She saw her own grief reflected in the faces of so many of the other women in the camps.

"How were you able to go on?" I asked her.

"You know it in an inner feeling that you have to be your own support, that you have to be your own morale. And the community helped. Grief is not as bad when it is shared." She continued, "I knew my husband went to fight for justice. That put the strength in me to live on and have the faith to fight. My hope is that the children that are the fruit of my marriage will have the opportunities that were not possible before. And that their opportunity was gained from a life that was given."

I looked at this woman who had faced such hardship with such tenacity. She was pointed in her comments about the culpability of the United States in her suffering. And yet she sat across the table from me with an attitude of acceptance. In my own American mentality, I thought she should at least throw the beer in my face, or break the bottle over my head. But she didn't. She talked and smiled and cried and laughed with me, with all the bumbling and rambling that goes with the territory of not speaking each other's language.

When she had told her story, I put down my pen, folded up my notebook, thanked her, and prepared to leave. But there was no mistaking her command to sit back down. We weren't finished yet.

She went and got us two warm Cokes and began to fire questions at my translator. Rosa wanted to know if I had children. I told her about my daughter. She wanted to know about my husband, about our house, about our work. My occupation as a psychologist confused her because she couldn't understand getting paid just to talk to people about what troubled them. As I answered her questions, I registered the irony of the enormous richness of my belongings against the relative poverty of my spirit. I was sitting with a woman for whom it would take three months of backbreaking work just to be able to buy the Victoria's Secret lingerie I was wearing under my Gap khakis and J. Crew work-shirt.

But Rosa had an openness, a freedom, and a spirit that I lacked. She smiled at me and said she had just one more question. She asked if the blonde streaks in my hair were real. I laughed, admitted they were not, and described how I take a little plastic cap with tiny holes, use a tiny metal pick to pull out small strands of hair, mix up a concoction of hair dyes, apply it to the strands, leave it on for an hour, and wash it out. She listened wide-eyed to the description. But as I described each step of the procedure, I felt worse and worse. My voice cracked and lowered and finally came to the point of breaking. When I finished I realized that I had just articulated, right out loud, the difference between Rosa and me. As I was talking, I began to know, in some way that I still don't totally understand, that my ability to wear great underwear and look like a blonde is related somehow to the fact that she can't. My riches are predicated upon her poverty. I was ashamed.

I slugged down a few sips of Coke and just sat there. I couldn't move, I couldn't speak, and I couldn't look into her eyes. Rosa moved over to me and covered my hand with hers. She uttered some words in Spanish. The only one I recognized was my name. She gazed straight at me with a slight smile and a look of wisdom that is only earned through suffering. And she whispered,

"Yo te perdono, Marta. Yo te perdono."

"I forgive you, Martha. I forgive you."

❧ LILIES OF THE VALLEY

THE PREPARATION for my first Holy Communion was just a horrible extension of my first confession. Even to an innocent seven-year-old, the contempt in which the teachers and the children of my parish held "public school" kids was glaring.

It wasn't the first time I had been an outsider. My father's changing FBI assignments necessitated several moves in several years, resulting in my attendance at three different kindergartens.

After first and second grade at the *same* school, I gratefully settled into the comfort of familiarity. I didn't care that I was only at the second-rate Burke Street (Public) School. I was well aware that the most essential, albeit narcissistic, distinction in the world was that of Catholic versus non-Catholic. I also knew that in the church's eyes, the very best public school couldn't begin to approach the very worst Catholic school. Whenever my parents were asked what school I attended, they always made it clear that Burke Street was only temporary because I was *on the waiting list,* indicating that the responsibility for my attendance at public school rested with the federal government and definitely not with them.

But I wanted to stay at Burke Street forever. I was tired of being different and new. I didn't want to walk down any more strange new halls behind strange new teachers who opened doors to rooms of strange new children. As if they had learned it in some teacher's handbook, public-school teachers always stood you in the front of the room, put one hand on your shoulder, called the children to attention, and issued those awful words, "Class, this is Martha Manning. She has just moved here from _____ (fill in last school attended)."

I never minded Sunday school, the consolation prize for public-school children. Since we were *all* outside the circle, we were spared painful comparisons. We sat for only one hour each week in the classrooms and seats of the "chosen," cramming into a short time what our counterparts could leisurely digest in an entire week. It wasn't until second grade, when the public-school kids were integrated with the Catholic school kids to receive the sacraments of penance and communion, that the different feeling returned, and I remembered how much I hated it.

Several days before the Saturday of our first communion, we ten public-school second-graders had to miss parts of our own school day to join the second-graders at Our Lady Queen of Angels for the final practice sessions. As a little kid, I could never tell which part of the ceremony was actual sacrament and which was pomp and circumstance. Certainly the nuns didn't differentiate it for us. *Everything* was critical—from the way we genuflected in absolute time with our partners, to the way we knelt at the communion rail, to the synchrony of standing, kneeling, and sitting in our seats. Somewhere in there you stuck out your tongue and received the Holy Eucharist, but the main energy was always directed at the surrounding show.

We had been well trained by Sister Miriam Jerome in the second-grade version of theology. We could answer by heart every question from our catechism.

After keeping us fueled with weekly doubts about whether we would ever be "prepared enough" for the sacraments, on the last Sunday before our first communion, she pronounced us as knowledgeable as our Queen of Angels School counterparts. But she was wrong. She taught us about the meaning of the sacrament, but she didn't teach us how to *perform* it.

Two days before "the day," my mother picked me up from Burke Street and delivered me to afternoon practice at our church, which, owing to the grandiosity of a previous pastor, looked like a little basilica. I had purposely worn a white blouse and plaid skirt, hoping I might blend in better with the other children's uniforms. But blue plaid is not green plaid. A white blouse is not a yellow blouse. And saddle shoes are not brown oxfords.

Despite the practice time listed in the announcement sent to my parents, it was clear that the Catholic school second-graders had already been practicing for some time. They were standing in the aisles, each girl matched with a boy partner. I learned quickly that my name was of absolutely no consequence, but my height had to be determined immediately. Sister Josephia, the commandant, sized me up and matched me to girls my size. This was not a task that allowed for vague estimations. Catholic processions somehow depended on exact size order. God forbid someone should have a growth spurt in the midst of the preparation period. The whole ceremony would have to be called off.

Sister made me stand back-to-back with several candidates until she was sure of my most accurate height placement. She then inserted me into the line like a book on a shelf. I was between a girl named Eileen, who looked at me as if I were crashing her birthday party, and a girl named Sally, who had to be nice to me because our mothers were friends. Eight girls were assigned to each pew, with each place marked by a bit of masking tape, resulting in perfectly straight rows—horizontally and vertically. As in all productions of this sort, the girls were on one side, the boys were on the other. I was proud that in such a short time I had found a place among the communicants and knew, quite literally, where I stood.

Once we were assigned our pews, we had to practice the grand procession into the church. I didn't really understand the concept of processions. Didn't we walk down that aisle every Sunday? What was so different about First Holy Communion Day?

I quickly learned what a big deal it was to accomplish all of the following—perfectly:

1 Keep time with the girls in your line *and* the boy across from you as you walk the length of the imposing aisle.

2 Keep your hands folded, pointed toward the ceiling.

3   Look straight ahead. Do not look around for family and friends.

4   Do not enter your pew until the preceding one has been filled.

5   Genuflect, part one: Bend down onto one knee (it must be the right one); remain there.

6   Make the sign of the cross: Right hand goes up, with first two fingers touching mid-forehead; down, with first two fingers touching mid-chest. Cross left with right hand touching left shoulder; cross right with right hand touching right shoulder; return to prior hand-praying position.

7   Genuflect, part two: Return to standing position.

8   Numbers 5 through 7 are to be done in synchrony with the boy partner.

9   Make a sharp, swift left at the same moment as your partner and turn precisely into your pew.

10 Remain standing directly in front of your piece of tape. Stare straight ahead, hands folded.

And that was just the first ten minutes.

God had been generous to me in the intellectual-skills department. Even at the age of seven, however, I knew that I had not been abundantly blessed in the area of motor skills. While I could see the procession rules in my head, their translation into action, particularly in forced rhythm with someone else, was damned difficult. I'd always end up making the sign of the cross while my knee was on the way down or on the way back up from the floor. I'd touch my right shoulder before my left. I was out of step with my partner, and I ended the day having failed repeatedly in navigating the ninety-degree left turn into the pew.

But, aside from minor chiding, I made it through the first afternoon unscathed. Sister Josephia's parting warning was the standard, "Just because you are only two days away from _____ (fill in specific ceremony or sacrament), don't think it's too late to cancel the entire thing, or to pull slackers from the list." I thought she was looking right at me. Even though I wasn't sure what a slacker was, I knew it wasn't good. I vowed to myself and God that I would work on the procession moves until I got them right, knowing that the next day was a full day of practice—the processional full court press.

First Holy Communion was a big deal in the fifties. People came from out of town. They gave great gifts. A special cake was ordered from a bakery. A large buffet dinner was planned. My mother had already set the table with the best of everything we owned and could borrow. My beautiful white communion dress, the most expensive dress I'd ever owned, hung from a ceiling lamp in the upstairs hallway, like a flag announcing an important event.

My mother made a major departure from her frugal ways. I didn't have to borrow another hand-me-down from our many neighbors, as I'd had to do with my Brownie uniform. My mother steered me away from all the frilly little dresses that looked like miniature bridal gowns. Instead, we found a crisp, elegant little dress that transcended the fashion of the moment and would always be, as my mother liked to say, a "classic"—meaning that every girl-child she had already produced, or would produce in the next decade, would wear it.

My new white shoes and ankle socks sat in the corner. The ensemble was waiting only for the finishing touches: a white veil and a white plastic pocketbook containing a white rosary and a white prayer book. These accessories were to be given at the very end of practice to each girl who was actually deemed ready to make her first communion. A lot was riding on my getting it right—for my parents and for me.

That night I enlisted the aid of my father in genuflecting, since he had come as close to the priesthood as any normal man I knew. He broke it all down for me. The sign of the cross, the genuflection, and then the combination of the two. I got it fairly quickly and then practiced until bedtime so that by the next day it would be almost instinctual. I could tell that my parents had absolutely no idea that I was in such serious danger of failing. They seemed slightly amused and touched by my insistence on getting everything down perfectly. I wanted to let them know that my name was only penciled in for communion, and that it wouldn't be written in ink unless I proved myself by the end of the next day.

The morning began easily. We practiced singing. Fortunately, I knew the melodies of the songs already, and, being an excellent reader, I could follow the printed words easily. I loved those songs—"Hail, Holy Queen, enthroned above / Hail, Mother of mercy and of love . . ." We sang about the seraphim and the cherubim, about Jesus loving the little children, about the benevolent God who keeps us from all harm. For the first time, I felt like I belonged. No one could out-Catholic me on those hymns.

But the late morning was a different story. It was time to practice processioning to the communion rail. We were told how to proceed out of the pew with our hands folded, how to walk solemnly up to the communion rail, kneel, take communion, bless ourselves, and return to our seats, kneel down, cover our face with our hands, and pray deeply until everyone was finished and we received the signal to rise.

It should have been quite simple. But I had practiced genuflecting so much that I reflexively went into a knee bend each time I got anywhere near a pew. Upon leaving my seat en route to the communion rail, I automatically genuflected (perfectly), creating a traffic jam of girls piling up in back of me, screwing up the tempo of the girls and boys' line, and creating a visible gap at the communion rail. By Sister Josephia's reaction, you would have thought I had just looked up disdainfully at the image of the crucified Christ and flipped him the finger.

She yanked me by the back of my blouse and pulled me from the line.

"You stupid, stupid girl," she hissed, careful not to raise her voice in the house of the Lord. "Weren't you paying attention?"

"Yes, but—"

"Yes?" she repeated as if she couldn't believe what I had said.

"Yes . . . but—" I stammered.

"Yes, SISTER," she replied.

I couldn't figure out why she was calling me "Sister."

"Yes?" I whispered again, both as an answer and a question.

"Yes, SISTER," she bellowed, startling even the other assistant nuns.

Everything stopped, shifting the entire focus to our interaction. On a hunch, I just repeated her words,

"Yes, Sister . . . "

With that she let go of my blouse and stood back, staring at me with disgust. "Do you consider yourself ready to receive our Lord Jesus Christ?"

"Yes," I answered, hoping like hell that I was right.

"Yes, SISTER!" she repeated. "Don't you owe our Lord more respect than your sloppiness for the great gift of his own body and blood?"

"Yes, but—"

"Yes, SISTER," she interrupted.

The woman might as well have been speaking ancient Arabic to me. Our conversation was half Gestapo interrogation and half "Who's on first?" by Abbott and Costello. I started to cry.

"What is the matter with you?" she asked mockingly.

"I don't feel good," I told her between gulps for air.

"I don't feel good, SISTER," she replied. "How don't you feel good?" she demanded.

"I think I'm . . ." She glared at me. ". . . Sister . . . going to throw up."

It was the only thing I could think of that would get me out of there. They wouldn't want the smell of fresh vomit violating the polished marble, the newly starched altar cloths, and the shining stained-glass windows. She turned me around to face the group. "Who knows this girl?" One kid from my street said that I lived next door to the Walsh family, who had at least seven children in the school. Ellen, a seventh grader, and my favorite, was dispatched to walk me home. She didn't drill me about what had happened. She just held my hand for the four-block walk, requesting only that if I threw up, I not do it on her.

My mother was surprised to see me so soon and worried when I told her I was sick. My grandparents and several aunts and uncles were due to arrive that evening. In her efficient diagnostic drill, she felt my head, looked down my throat, and palpated my glands. She attributed my red eyes to allergy and told me to lie down for a while, promising she would bring me ginger ale. How could I tell this kind woman that I'd just been banished? That all her silver polishing and vacuuming and errands were wasted? That I was the only girl too stupid to receive Jesus? I knew I couldn't. I cringed every time the phone rang, struggling to hear the condemnation I knew was coming.

After a half hour my mother came to my door, told me I looked a bit better, and asked if I wanted to go with her to our friend Mary Nolan's house to pick up some serving dishes for the buffet. I couldn't confess yet to the futility of the trip. My brother was still in school and my two sisters were with a baby-sitter, so my mother could run her errands. The chance to ride alone with my mother anywhere was so unusual that I agreed, hoping I could work up the nerve to gently tell her the truth in private. On the ride over, she asked how practice went. "Not too good," I mumbled.

"Why not?"

"The sister said I didn't pay attention. . . . And I'm bad at lines."

"That's nonsense," my mother declared, never betraying a bit of concern at the gravity of these deficits.

For the remainder of the ride she pointed out the warmth and fragrance of early May, pronouncing her confidence that my communion day would be beautiful. When we arrived at Mary's house, she told me to sit on the steps while she ran in. While I waited, I saw the school bus slow down and stop at the corner. Several second-grade girls and boys were among the lot that tumbled out onto the sidewalk. My worst fears were confirmed. Each of them carried an identical box, except the girls' were white and the boys' were brown. Some of the boxes had been opened on the bus. Girls were trying on their veils and examining their white plastic pocketbooks. I didn't have a box. It was true; I was off the list.

My mother emerged from the house with Mary, their arms full of dishes and silver. Mary, who'd known me since I was born, threw her arms around me and sang, "I can't wait to see you tomorrow." I smiled and nodded as the voice inside me said, *There isn't going to be tomorrow.* My mother turned toward the house and yelled back over her shoulder, "Wait a second, I forgot something." In less than a minute she returned with a homemade bouquet of lilies of the valley from Mary's backyard. Little upside-down bells of flowers, delicate in design but powerful in fragrance. They were wrapped at the base with a wet napkin, which was covered with an old piece of aluminum foil. When my mother presented them to me, I thought she meant for me just to hold them for the ride home.

"Don't you like them?" she asked, as we pulled out onto the street.

"They're pretty," I answered flatly. My mother looked a bit hurt.

"I thought they would make a beautiful first-communion bouquet," she offered.

Yeah, I thought, for someone *making* her first communion.

Finally, finally, I voiced my doubt.

"What if there isn't going to *be* a first communion?" I asked.

"The weather forecast says it will be a day exactly like today. Besides, they always have a rain plan."

"No, Mom," I corrected her. "What if . . . like there . . . was going to be a communion, but a *person* wasn't going to be allowed to be in it?"

"A person like you?" she asked.

"Yeah, a person like me."

"Well, I wouldn't let that happen to a person like you," she said, clearly indicating that she had delivered her first and last words on the subject. But she looked at my face and saw that it wasn't enough. I could not put into words the combination of humiliation and guilt that I felt. I couldn't tell her about that nun, in her mean black-and-whiteness, who made me feel more like a child of Satan than a child of God. I couldn't tell her that I had failed, truly, completely, and publicly, and that the consequences of my failure reached far beyond me—to my parents, my brothers and sisters, my grandparents already on the road from Boston, the buffet guest list. To the wasted dress and cake, to the presents that would need to be returned, not to mention the serious retardation of my spiritual development. "Smell your flowers, Martha. I promise you. Everything will be all right."

So I smelled my flowers, sniffing them first, and then inhaling. And for the first time in my life, I consciously experienced the promise of Christ—that love will always conquer hate. In that small bouquet, I knew that the power of my mother's love was greater than the disapproval of the meanest nun. I was not on my own, as I sometimes feared. My mother was there. I could have confessed to farting at the benediction, picking my nose in the procession, or puking on an old nun's shoe. And ultimately, it wouldn't have mattered. I understood, in my guts, what I had rotely memorized for months. Jesus loves us like all those little children crawling all over him in those pictures. Jesus loves us when we're good. He loves us when we're bad. But, most basically, he loves us just because we *are*.

I realized that the nuns could cross my name off their list and I would still wear my beautiful white dress, smile for my pictures, cut my cake, and open my gifts. It was a done deal, which a couple of screwups could never negate.

When we returned home, my mother picked up a wrinkled grocery bag that had been left on the front steps. I ran to the kitchen, put my flowers in water, and took the steps to my bedroom two at a time to place them on my bureau. My mother followed me to my room and smiled as she handed over the wrinkled paper bag. I reached inside and found the box, the special communion box. I opened up the package with the veil and handed it to my mother to hang with my dress. Then I opened the purse— white grained plastic, with a shoulder strap and a fake gold clasp that twisted to open and close. Inside was a children's prayer book, covered with fake white mother-of-pearl; it had a picture of Jesus inside and a place for my name. The pages were smooth and each illustration shone. The edges of the pages were trimmed with gold and, like the missals of grown-ups, it had satin markers for keeping special places. The rosary beads matched the prayer book cover, white pearl-like beads with a silver crucifix, so slippery that the five decades of the rosary could roll off your fingers as quickly as they fell from your tongue. There was a little cheap silver medal of the Blessed Mother and several holy cards of Jesus, Mary, and the saints.

That night, as I received my solid gold religious medals, engraved necklaces, bracelets, and savings bonds from my relatives, my mother tried to point out their great value relative to the packet of white communion junk that cost no more than a couple of bucks. But she didn't need to instruct me on value. The bells in the jelly jar in my bedroom and the cheap white communion paraphernalia were my prizes. They were the priceless symbols of the redemptive power of love.

The next bright morning, in the midst of 119 children so white in the sun that we seemed to shimmer and merge, I knew, without question, that I belonged. When the priest actually placed the round wafer on my outstretched tongue, it was almost redundant. I had already received my first communion. My mother was my priest, the flowers were my Eucharist, and I was the stumbling, sorry recipient, overwhelmed at my own unworthiness, shaky in my faith, but loved completely in spite of it. No, maybe loved completely *because* of it.

It was the best thing my mother ever gave me. And she remembers not a second of it. Nothing. My assessment of her finest hour of mothering doesn't even fall within her list of the best hundred things she's done for me. But unconditional love is like that. It is given so freely, so easily, that we forget to count the costs.

🌸 GULLS

IT IS EARLY MORNING and I am sitting at a small desk in front of a picture window of a seedy motel on the beach. Fishermen's lines are stacked in the sand along the shoreline. The gulls are conversing back and forth. One gull sounds like it is laughing hysterically. No, it's two gulls. One is absolutely still and silent. The other one is all action and shouting. Then I realize that they are screwing—the male atop the female, squawking and flailing; the female looking silently, stoically, indifferently still, bearing his weight and motion. Now they stand together, still and silent, one in front of the other, staring, as I am, at the sea.

It is unclear whether this is the seagulls' version of smoking a cigarette or whether, like me, they're just trying to figure out what to do next.

Chasing Grace

Late yesterday afternoon, a tall man with skinny sunburnt legs held a slice of bread up in the air. At least twenty gulls converged and circled around him, slowly daring to come closer, but stopping themselves short at some invisible barrier just as they were about to reach his hand. I could see them hovering in the air, the tension working in their wings to keep them simultaneously aloft and stationary so that they could figure out what to do with this offering. As the man dropped his hand, the gulls descended with it, only to fly up immediately as he raised the bread back up into the air. Finally, one reckless gull swooped in from the safety of the periphery, snatched the bread from the man's hand, and savored the entire piece for itself. I thought that witnessing the rewarded bravery of a compatriot would embolden the other gulls. But it didn't. The man reached into a plastic bag and pulled out another slice. The gulls resumed their hovering, totally absorbed by the contents of this hand in the air. They were stuck somewhere between hunger and fear, need and risk. There was a line, invisible to me, that they dared not cross, even if it meant only staring at the bread rather than swallowing it.

I wanted to scream at the foolish, frightened gulls, Go for it, you idiots! That hand is there to feed you, not to hurt you. But then I laughed. Not at them. At me. I am constantly hovering around the edges of the things I want or need from the outstretched arms of the people I love. I expend enormous amounts of energy just flitting about, all my effort tied up in the wanting, so that little is left for the getting.

Something keeps getting in the way of my taking what is offered. I watch it. I flirt with the possibilities of it. I covet it. But I so rarely take the big chance of just swooping in and gratefully snatching it from an outstretched hand. If I never claim it as mine, I avoid all risk, all responsibility. The problem is that when I play by those rules, I also lose out on the prize. I am the stoic gull, who hungers silently for the flailing, squawking pleasures of

her mate and hovers eternally around her own satisfaction, afraid
to swoop in and claim it.

❧ GENEROSITY

A FEW YEARS AGO, my daughter needed a pair of shoes
for my sister's wedding. It was an eleventh-hour operation, so typical of our household. The night before the wedding we discovered that she had outgrown her good shoes and couldn't even do
a wicked-stepsister squeeze into mine.

Hoping to avoid shopping malls, which I despise, I dragged
her to the local discount shoe outlet. I say "dragged," because my
fourteen-year-old and I were of two absolutely different minds
when it came to shopping. She considered shopping close to an
art form. For me it was, and still is, about as entertaining as scrap-
ing the soap scum off bathroom tiles.

While I had always taken great pride in getting a piece of
clothing as quickly and cheaply as possible, my daughter at that
age sneered at anything that did not have a designer label and an
astronomical price tag. Predictably, she hated all the cheap shoes.
The one pair for which she demonstrated the least disgust was
unavailable in her size.

In the interest of time, I relented and drove to the local mall.
On the way I recognized a sight that had become familiar over
several months. In the parking lot of a fast-food restaurant, a
number of women stood in a long line. Many held a child in one
arm and an empty box or bag in the other. As I sat at the stoplight, I was impressed with the camaraderie among the women in
this line that had no apparent beginning or end.

What were they waiting for? The question occupied me while
I waited for the light to change. But once the women disappeared
from my sight, they left my mind, as I turned back to thoughts of
my own plans.

My daughter made a beeline for the shoe department at Macy's. I felt dizzy at the astounding selection of shoes, as well as the hordes of women swarming around them. We were competitors, with the prize going to the most aggressive. The only thing we shared was our impatience. We looked at our watches. We sighed loudly. We muttered under our collective breath. We flashed plastic cards. We sized up the competition, mentally designating as obnoxious only those women who were even more demanding than ourselves. We were fully prepared to spend a lot of money for shoes that looked almost exactly like the pairs we were already wearing.

All of a sudden, it felt absurd to be in that place, jostling with those women, frantic in the pursuit of one more thing. I looked at my daughter who, in the midst of all that merchandise, seemed close to a mystical experience.

Eventually, my daughter found some shoes. We surrendered a great deal of money to Macy's and headed for the exit. In that uniquely adolescent way of communicating disdain she said, "All right, go ahead. Give the speech." I was preoccupied with finding my keys and not following the conversation well.

"What speech?" I asked absentmindedly. She then delivered my usual social-justice diatribe, complete with painfully good imitations of my gestures and inflections. It was then that I realized these sermons meant absolutely nothing to her. She filed them away in the same part of her brain where she stores my lectures on her messy room and the importance of good oral hygiene. I felt defeated.

We drove in silence. The women were still there. I was immediately interested in their shoes. Some wore flat, serviceable shoes— shoes that are good for all occasions, shoes that support long walks and long waits. Others wore plastic sandals and flip-flops over bare feet despite the cool autumn temperatures.

Several days later our neighborhood newsletter, which I never read, arrived in the mail. I noticed a blurb on the last page recruiting volunteers to pick up food and deliver it to people in the parking lot near my house. I've had these moments of private co-incidence before. The ones where I feel creepy and self-conscious because I never really articulated the question, so how could I be getting the answer? At these times I usually squint, look toward the general direction of heaven, and ask, "Are you talking to *me?*" The fullness of the silent response that follows can only be described as a strong spiritual kick in the ass.

I volunteered the whole family. The first night we worked distributing food I was surprised by the ease with which my daughter performed whatever task she was assigned. This was not the material girl of the shopping mall. I realized that I had to give her more chances to be generous.

I remember when I was a child and my father had been out "working on a case" all night. He called in the very early morning to announce that he was bringing home a family that had just escaped from Cuba. We would give them breakfast while the authorities were trying to find sanctuary for them.

My mother, who already had her hands full with six young children, did not look at all pleased with the prospect of entertaining strangers at 5:00 A.M. But she quickly shook off her annoyance and mobilized us in a series of tasks. She smoothed the good linen cloth on the dining-room table. She set out the good crystal, china, and silver—items reserved for major holidays.

When we complained that she was going overboard for people we didn't even know, she sat us down and said in her best cut-the-bullshit voice, "Listen, these people left their home and country two days ago with nothing but the clothes on their backs. They know little about where they are and even less about where they're going. They deserve to have the best meal we can give them, and I don't want to hear one more word about it!"

So we set the table and stirred the orange juice. We made the toast and fried the bacon. My mother sent us in search of clothes and toys for the children, requiring small acts of kindness from each of us in deciding which belongings to give away. When they arrived, she led us in greeting them with great warmth. She didn't know a word of Spanish, but you never would have known it.

No one would have guessed we pulled off that meal in less than an hour. Our two families squeezed together around the dining-room table. The considerable language gap was bridged by the pleasures of food and the delights of children.

I had no understanding of the political context in which all of this was occurring, but it didn't really matter. All I knew was that my parents had done something good and that they had let us do it too.

Those early opportunities for generosity echo much more re-soundingly in my memory than any of my parents' words. So tonight, as my daughter and I hand out dented cans of soup to lines of women who've been standing too long in flat, plain shoes, I will remember the redundancy of language and spare her my righteous litanies.

❧ WOMEN AT TABLES

WE MEET as we have for fifteen years—one evening each month. Dinner and conversation. Eight of us in all, survivors of the quest for a doctorate, now trying to make peace with the prize. It is church with these women. Giving and taking. Breaking the bread and sharing the wine. Breaking the words and sentences of our lives into bite-sized pieces—each giving to her own capac-ity and taking according to her needs.

We do not linger long on the words that define us by our work. Instead, our conversations break free. We still admit to watching fine young men as they emerge from pickup trucks at the 7–Eleven, balancing our appreciation of them with the grudging knowledge that, at our ages, we have moved from "honey" to "ma'am" in these boys' vocabularies. We battle ourselves, the same stern critics who didn't like the way we looked then, and certainly don't now. We shake our heads at our vanity and admit that we should have been happier with what we had. But we realize that we will say the very same thing in twenty years, when the way we look right now begins to seem pretty good and we will kick ourselves once again; that we are only able to call ourselves lovely in retrospect.

The hurdles of graduate school that initially united us are now replaced by greater difficulties. Despite our skills at charting other people's lives, we never quite pictured these pains for our own. Our parents are dying, often slowly and painfully. The sorrows of infertility are frequent and deep. We delineate the technologies of conception, celebrating their successes and mourning their failures. We have learned the vastness of the perilous road that stretches from conception to birth and have suffered numerous losses along the way. We confide our marriages, celebrate beginnings, anticipate endings, or just document the simultaneous complexity and simplicity of men. We nourish ourselves at this table so that we can meet the endless hungers—of our patients, our children, our husbands, our lovers.

But "women's group" is more than just a place to talk about other people. It is the place we come month after month to remember or to realize who *we* are. All the frailties masked so masterfully in our therapist's chairs are invited to come out of hiding. And if these frailties are not loved, then they are at least always tolerated.

This table is where we bring our morbid fears about the evils of the world. It is the place where we tell the things that make us look foolish. It is the place where we come to cry and no one jumps in with cheap advice, or looks away. We just sit with one another, and the pain doesn't go away exactly, but it loses its gravity as it floats around the room and connects us with one another. And in that moment the pain is less, because it is shared. We cry one another's tears, and together we curse the heartless bastards or the careless gods. We hold a hand, stroke a face, or pour a good stiff drink. And in the middle of the absolutely low-downest tar pits of distress, we can leave it all for a moment . . . and laugh. Not a denying, deflecting, let's-forget-about-this laugh, but a laugh that makes it clear that there is always another side to sorrow.

We are encircled, these women and I. Love surrounds us and transcends our many differences. Love is there in the sadness when pain is all we know and the hurt comes without knocking and we feel unprepared to receive it. It is there in the fear as we keep vigilant watch for the bogeyman, the monsters in the closet, the terrors we feel for the children who are breaking free from us in a world so full of evil. It is there in the pleasure of one another, and in the realization of the boundlessness of that joy—when we can laugh so hard that we cry. And when we can cry so hard that we laugh.

Women's group is where we learn about growing up and growing older. About how wisdom is good, but why does it always have to hurt so bad? It is the place where so much gets done with so little to show for it, continually confusing the men in our lives who still cannot comprehend the concept of "just talking" for hours.

Our talk is our prayer. It is our faith. When we share those deep lonely corners and those brilliant expanses that fight for ascendancy in our souls, we acknowledge the possibility of divinity among us, of the sacredness of this constellation we call "women's group." We recognize our connections to women from the beginning of time. Women have rarely known primacy in temples or churches, and so we continue to find it at *other* altars, with our sisters, who have *never* lacked for words, only for voices and volume.

Martha Manning

❧ SHORTEN THE ROAD

SUFFERING IS THE CURRENCY of psychotherapy. As a young clinical psychologist, I assumed that because I had distinguished myself in making it through the trial by fire of graduate school, I was eminently qualified to heal people's suffering.

What I didn't know was that the most important things to know about suffering aren't taught in any classroom. They are learned in "real life," the practicum that never ends.

There seem to be two levels of suffering. There's the suffering itself. And then there is the almost universal sense of isolation that comes with the territory of suffering.

The sense of being set apart in one's pain is rooted in two places. One has to do with the hard but true fact that no one can walk our road for us. When people tell me that in their suffering they "feel so alone," I don't rush, anymore, to point out the ways in which they are not alone. I admit that on a certain level, they are right. They *are* alone. Nobody but a woman can feel the sting of sexism firsthand. No one can feel the terror of homelessness unless he's lived on the streets. No one knows the horrors of chemotherapy unless she's had cancer. No one can know what it feels like to see suicide as attractive until he's lived in hell. Millions of people have experienced, are experiencing, or will experience these things in their lifetimes. But despite the numbers, their unique experience in these events is a story that sometimes needs telling, and retelling, for healing to occur.

Sometimes it is so hard to hear those stories. I often have great difficulty just *being* with people in the constancy and complexity of their pain. It makes me feel guilty, responsible, and inept. It scares me to really look at another person in pain because it reminds me of my own vulnerability. It's also extremely hard to realize that in some situations there is absolutely nothing to *do*. The *doing* is in the *being* with another person.

Sometimes the first thing I want to say, "I know just how you feel," is the last thing the other person wants to hear. When people tell me they know how I feel, I want to punch them. It feels like they are trying to diminish my hurt, spare me from talking about it, and themselves from having to hear it, because it's already been said, it's already been felt. I need to tell my stories and my patients need to tell theirs. There is no *standard* experience of pain, no unit of measurement against which we can evaluate suffering. And for that reason, there is no standard story.

All I have to do to remember that is to wait for the usual fifty or sixty minutes in my OB-GYN's office. The times I've spent there recounting pregnancy, labor, and delivery details are the closest I've ever been to sitting around a campfire swapping stories. Most of the details are the same. We all missed our periods. We got due dates. We felt tired. We threw up. We cried at AT&T commercials. We gained a lot of weight. We had near-mystical experiences with our little boarders. We took classes. We dilated, we effaced, our water broke, we went into labor. We cursed our mates, our doctors, our mothers, and any other human person who made this sound like a natural, wonderful thing to do. We pushed, we gave birth, we fell in love, we nursed, we went home, we never slept. But each woman's experience of every one of those details is uniquely her own. The food that makes one woman lose her lunch is another woman's dietary salvation. The very same doctor can be the midwife of God or the prince of darkness, depending on what the woman needed and what he or she was able to provide.

But I have also learned that I don't have to go through every type of pain to make me a credible listener. I have no intention of becoming an alcoholic so that I can better understand those members of my family, friends, and patients who struggle with alcoholism. I pray that I am spared from that, and all the other hardships that would make me closer kin to other sufferers. In my own way, I have suffered long and hard, and it has taught me that there are also universals of pain that can bridge the gap between my experience (or lack of it) and another person's very different pain.

In the experience of disaster, it doesn't much matter if you felt an earthquake and I felt a tornado. It doesn't matter that one felt the road ripple under her feet and the other felt the power of the darkest circles of wind with strength beyond imagination. We both know what it's like for life to swing out of control, to lose all sense of balance and perspective, to free-fall from complacency, to lose hope, to be awed by destruction, to wonder if order will ever return. We both know the humbling feeling of being small and helpless. From that, we can face each other's difficulties, be they the nightmares that curse our sleep or the fears that haunt our days.

The essence of the singular struggle with suffering is the same. It is the dogfight between spirit and strength on the one side and fear and resignation on the other. We all know the universals of the struggle: it's hard, it's lonely, it's scary, and it takes too damn long.

I have always loved the classic memoir *To School Through the Fields*, in which Alice Taylor relates the old Irish legend of a ruler who wished to leave his kingdom to the cleverest of his three sons. He took the first son on a long journey. On the way he said, "Son, shorten the road for me." The oldest son was overwhelmed by the task, gave up, and they returned home. The king embarked on the same journey with the second son and said again, "Son, shorten the road for me." Like his older brother, the boy was daunted by the request, gave up, and they too returned home. The king then took the youngest son on the long journey. Once again he said,

"Son, shorten the road for me." The youngest son launched into a story so long and so engrossing that before the king knew it, he had completed the long journey.

It has taken me years past my clinical training as a psychologist to realize that, no matter how good I am, I can't lessen the number of miles on the road, even for people I love like crazy. I can't walk that long way for those people. But like the king on the road, I know that just having a companion on some part of the road can make the long, lonely walk seem shorter, and make the journeys, however difficult, infinitely more bearable.

Confirmation

I believe

🌺 *You got a nice white dress and a party*
on your Confirmation.
You got a brand new soul and a cross of gold.
But Virginia, they didn't give you
quite enough information . . .

> —Billy Joel,
>   "Only the Good Die Young"

❧ ICE CREAM

I HAD TO BE resourceful to spend time alone with my father.

Weeknights were out, because he came home so late. If I wanted to get up early, he would walk me to school on his way to the Long Island Railroad stop a bit farther down the road.

My father sometimes worked undercover, ferreting out spies in Chinatown and the Bowery in New York City. Not the smooth type of undercover I'd seen in the movies, where the guy looks rich and suave and sexy. My father looked like a bum. And not a Halloween-type bum, where the person appears basically clean and middle-class underneath. My father looked like he'd been a bum forever.

One morning I was up and ready for school early, so my father suggested that we walk together. It was one of those bum days when he looked really awful. I declined, but he wouldn't accept my refusals. Having already been up for a few hours, my father was quite chatty and cheerful. It would have been a perfect time to have him all to myself. But I didn't want it *that* bad. I tried not to walk in step with him, hoping that passersby would not associate us. I marched quickly ahead, but my father was a runner and could effortlessly outdistance me. When I deliberately stalled, he slowed his pace accordingly.

As we approached the school, I could see the older boys playing softball on the field that I would have to pass to get to the girls' section of the playground. I suggested to my father that he might want to cross the street, since the train station was on the other side. He shrugged and insisted that he was happy to walk past the school and then cross over. I wished there were trapdoors in sidewalks so that really embarrassed people could just fall right out of view. I made a lot of room between my father and me, so that maybe it would look like he was walking beside me, not with me. But then, at the point where our paths were about to diverge, he did the unthinkable. My mangy deadbeat father leaned over and kissed me good-bye.

He walked on. I fixed my eyes on the ground and walked briskly toward the girls' playground. A boy yelled out, "Is that your *father?*" What could I say? He was an eighth-grader. I was unsure of myself and desperate to make a good impression. I gave an emphatic "No!" and then threw in, "Of course not!" because it sounded like a smart thing to say.

Another eighth-grader from my neighborhood yelled, "Manning, you liar! That's your father."

Someone else exclaimed, "God, what a bum!"

"He is *not* a bum," I shouted indignantly. I wasn't being altruistic and protecting my father; I was protecting myself. I was getting to the age at which parents were inherently embarrassing. They didn't need to do anything more than breathe to mortify you in front of other kids. And my father had gone way past breathing.

"My father is an FBI agent," I proclaimed haughtily.

"Oh yeah, then why does he look like that?" challenged a seventh-grader.

"He's on a *case*," I sniffed. "He's working *undercover.*"

All the big guys started to imitate me.

One guy leered, "You know what FBI means, don't you?"

I stuck out my chin and replied royally, "It means Federal Bureau of Investigation."

"No, it doesn't," he sneered. "It means Fat Boys Incorporated."

Then the rest of the preadolescent Neanderthals repeated it over and over in singsong voices and laughed me onto the farthest end of the sprawling playground.

I was mad at them, but I was madder at my father, who was obviously aware of how critical appearance was in *his* line of work but had no comprehension of its importance in mine. I refused all further walks to school. We were limited to weekends.

Spending weekend time with my father usually meant tagging along. There was a basic formula to our outings: I sat through something boring and when that was finished, my father and I did something fun. I went with him to get his hair cut at a place that had a real candy-cane barber pole and the barber let kids pick Dum-dum lollipops out of a wooden box labeled FOR GOOD GIRLS AND BOYS—just like at my pediatrician's office. I always wondered whether there was an equivalent box marked FOR BAD BOYS AND GIRLS and loved to imagine rotten children reaching in and getting their little hands stuck in mousetraps. It took me as long to choose a lollipop as it did for my father to get his haircut. Dum-dums had more choices than any other kind of lollipop, and at my age, it felt critical to make the absolutely right choice.

I watched my father play tennis, and he took me to Howard Johnson's, where I got strawberry milkshakes and he didn't even get mad when I was playing with my straw and accidentally blew milkshake onto the waitress's white uniform. I shivered through his pickup hockey games with the local college and high-school boys. It was there that I learned not only how to skate like a boy, but how to use every swear word known to man, alone and in creative combinations. I deflated in the heat, inhaling gasoline fumes, as my father tried, unsuccessfully, to start the outboard motor on our boat. He'd pull the motor rope and curse, pull the rope and curse. The motor would tease him with a brief turnover and then stop, leaving my father ready to tear out what little hair he had left. On those long mornings at the dock, as my father sputtered more than the motor, I found myself wondering about the wisdom of putting a loaded gun into the hands of a man so mechanically inept.

The best times were when he took me out for ice cream. Not one of those everyone-pile-in-the-station-wagon-for-Carvel's kind of deals, where my brother and I got yelled at for biting off the bottoms of our cones and slurping our ice cream upside down, even though we loved to and never made a mess. We weren't allowed to do it because we would "set a bad example" for the little kids. The prohibition took a significant amount of pleasure from the experience.

When I went alone with my father for ice cream, it was altogether different. I'd change from my play clothes into a skirt and blouse and wear my Sunday shoes and good socks. My father changed from his weekend clothes to a sports coat and tie. He brought two empty suitcases down from the attic and handed me the little plaid one. Then we took a long ride to the airport. I loved airports. I enjoyed sizing people up and trying to figure out where they were going, based on what they looked like. My father wore sunglasses and held my hand as we walked though the terminal. I thought the sunglasses part was neat and slipped on my Mickey Mouse sunglasses, but my father made me put them away.

Every now and then, he'd check in at a counter or tell me to stand still while he made a phone call. After we'd walked for a while, my father found an empty bench that looked out on the airplanes arriving and departing. I sat down with my little plaid suitcase. He told me to wait right there until he came back and not to say anything to anyone. I watched the planes, the people coming through the gate, the beautiful stewardesses. Grandmotherly women passed by and told me I was "adorable" or "such a big girl" to be waiting on my own. They asked me questions. I obeyed my father's orders and gave them nothing but a smile.

I don't know how long I waited. But after a while he always came back, carrying his empty suitcase. He'd make a few more phone calls with a really serious look on his face. Then he'd smile, and I knew it was finally time for ice cream.

I understood that we were on an adventure, but I had no idea what kind. And in that special way that little kids have of trusting adults, neither did I care. It never occurred to me that it was the least bit odd to be carrying two empty suitcases. I never questioned the fact that we drove forty-five minutes to Idlewild airport for ice cream when there was a place within walking distance of our house. It didn't seem strange that my father kept putting money in the phone for calls he could have made for free before, or after, our airport excursion. Why did he always leave me alone, swinging my legs, looking around and counting planes? The only thing that ever bothered me at *all* was that my father was allowed to wear his sunglasses in the airport but I wasn't allowed to wear mine.

There were so many times like that in my childhood. Times when, in retrospect, I see that the strangest things went on, but I filtered them through the reactions I observed in grown-ups, under the illusion that what they showed on their faces was what they actually felt. When Thomas Kelly's mother threw deck furniture overboard in the middle of the Long Island Sound and no grown-up screamed or fainted, it must have been all right. When my uncle water-skied with a kid on his shoulders and a beer in his hand, it must have been fine. If, in the middle of a Labor Day party, my father carried Mrs. Lowry around in an empty garbage can where she then got stuck, and no one looked alarmed, so be it.

The hard thing for kids is that the craziest stuff often gets the least overt reaction from adults, leaving kids very confused about which things are big deals and which things don't matter. Kids have no interpreter to help them observe grown-ups and say things like, "See how that father smacked his boy across his face? That's not normal. It's terrible." Or "Listen to the way that girl's mother talks to her. You won't find the harm in the words. You'll hear it in the tone." Or "Even though your parents are yelling really loud right now, and you're scared they'll get a divorce, this kind of fight is normal. And it has nothing to do with you." An interpreter would have saved us pain, just by spelling things out and making the strange life outside of childhood a bit clearer.

But there are other times I am glad there are still vestiges of my childhood innocence. I loved it when, at the age of thirty, the association between ice cream and airports popped back into my head. On a long layover in Chicago, I reached across an ice-cream counter for a chocolate cone and then found a seat to kill time and watch planes. As I swung my crossed leg back and forth and slurped the ice cream, my body remembered something my mind had forgotten. The memory startled me initially. The little-girl me came face-to-face with my grown-up self. I can still hear the horrified grown-up in me yelling, *Jesus Christ, Dad used me as a cover for FBI surveillance!* But then I hear the little girl with the empty plaid suitcase and the Mickey Mouse sunglasses answering, *Yeah . . . so?* as she raises her chocolate ice-cream cone and chomps a huge dripping bite off the bottom.

❧ BELIEVING

WHEN MY DAUGHTER was eight, she stopped believing in Santa Claus. Well, she didn't all of a sudden stop. You don't stop believing in Santa the way you stop believing in a person who suddenly and cruelly betrays you. She just let the doubt creep in over time until the magic couldn't even it out.

The magic held out for an amazingly long time. I was five when I said to my mother, "There's no such thing as Santa, is there?" She answered, "No."

That pretty much ended it right there.

But Keara was different. She had one foot in reality, fascinated with facts, numbers, trivia, quotations. When contemplating which part she would get in the second-grade school play, she told me, "Mom, there are no small parts, only small actors." An eight-year-old Anglophile, she dressed for Halloween as her idol, Queen Elizabeth I, and then stayed up half the night wracked with fear that she might be mistaken by her third-grade classmates for Mary Queen of Scots.

But her other foot was firmly embedded in fantasy or, as she called it, "dream thinking." Those two parts of her existed entirely peacefully in a mind that was simultaneously adept at processing information and completely tolerant of that which made absolutely no logical sense.

The previous winter, after reading an article in the *Washington Post* about the ways in which parents disabuse their children of the notion of Santa, Keara had stomped down the stairs and sputtered out an angry command for me to read the article. At first, I thought she was mad at me for stringing her along all those years. But to my relief she was furious with the writer, the publisher, and every other human being who had had a hand in delivering such slander in an otherwise respectable newspaper. She wrote an outraged letter (complete with spelling errors) to the editor of the *Washington Post:*

> Dear Newspaper,
>   There is a story in your newspaper by Karen Timmons. It is the truth about JOLLY SAINT NICK. I am very dissapointed that you would let a story like this be put in your newspaper. It says that parents are lying about St. Nick and it says that there is no such thing and I OBJECT. I think the person is just showing that they do not belive in the magic of St. Nick. I think you should never put an story like this again.
>   From,
>   Keara Depenbrock
>   Age 7
>   A CHILD!
>
> P.S. I'm shoked but have a Mery Cristmas.

It would have been the perfect time to sit her down and explain the facts to her, but I just couldn't. Mostly for her sake, partly for mine. Christmas is so much better with a child who believes.

But in her eighth year, the magic finally lost out. She decided that if every single kid on her school bus didn't believe, then it really was time to reconsider her position. I'm so sad to see believing go. I wanted to push the fantasy just one more year, but she asked me so directly. It was time to tell the truth.

What else do you stop believing when you give up on Santa Claus? In one day, Santa, the elves, and the reindeer bit the dust. The Easter Bunny and the Tooth Fairy wouldn't be far behind. As I put her to bed that night, she demanded a rundown of all the children we knew who probably still believed in Santa. Suddenly seeing herself as part of the "enlightened ones," she felt a bit superior to the believers who were about her age, and protective of the fantasies of the many little children in her life.

I rubbed her back in silence as she settled under her comforter, with her pillows in absolutely correct formation so that she could see the moon from her window.

I couldn't help thinking, Don't always let what is real win out over what is magic. Let them live together inside you. Take joy from the things that give you pleasure, even though most of them can't be quantified or explained. You and your dream-thinking have let the magic back into my life, too. Sharing the fantasy of Santa brought me back to when I was a little girl. Back to when the tree we got was the absolutely most beautiful, the waiting was interminable, and the hope was immeasurable. I loved sharing that with you. I hope that you will find some piece of magic in your life that you can always grab hold of, particularly when the toll of reality is more than you can bear.

With the fall of Santa, I wonder when I, too, will lose my magic with you. When will I stop being the mother who can make a bump better with a kiss, a sorrow softer with a tickle, and a nightmare disappear with a backrub? As you began pointing out the flaws in the store-Santas we saw tonight—"What a fake beard." "There's stuffing in his stomach." "He's wearing makeup."—I wondered when I will fall from grace. When will I shift from "Mommy" to "Mooottthheeerrr"? When will my singing in the car turn from entertaining to embarrassing? When will my clothes, my hair, my mannerisms, and just the basic fact that we inhabit the same planet become a public source of humiliation?

It's coming. You don't know it yet. But I do. Santa Claus, the Easter Bunny, the monsters in your closet, your guardian angel, and the Tooth Fairy will all have to shove over on the bench to make room for me. And together we will watch the rest of the game from the sidelines, rooting you on but never being quite as central to the play as we are right now.

We are growing up, you and I. Santa and his friends have left our house, but please believe me when I tell you that the magic will always prevail—in Dad, in me, and especially, my sweet child, in you.

✣ MY GOD

THE FOUNDATIONS of my faith were laid down early, within the institution of "church." But often, what I learn about the *application* of that faith comes to me most powerfully outside church walls. Many times it occurs in places that claim no religious affiliation but, for me, provide constant reminders and reassurances that God is very much present in this troubled world.

Several years ago, I visited a home for babies with HIV. These babies were born into homelessness and, often, motherlessness. But there was nothing institutional about the place. Everything about it said "home." It was the sheer numbers of everything—five high chairs, five cribs, stacks of diapers—that let me know I wasn't in an ordinary house. The gloves by each changing table, the instructions on refrigerators and in bathrooms, and the shelves full of medicines underscored the vulnerability of these children.

The memory of those babies and their caretakers has come back to me often. There is something about them that makes me consider my relationship (or lack of one) with God.

By the time a new baby enters the home, he or she has usually spent considerable time as a boarder baby in a hospital, often waiting a long time for special placement. A hospital, however wonderful, is no place for children to thrive. Development slows down. Many of the babies adopt a passivity about the world. The light goes out in their eyes. They want only the basics, because that is all they know. Unlike my daughter, who demanded *more* attention as she got older, these babies demand *less.* They form tenuous connections to the people who care for them, and they make no assumptions about permanent attachments.

So often, that is precisely my relationship with God. I can usually acknowledge God's existence, but only in an abstract and disconnected way. I cannot bring myself to believe that God is truly "mine." Unlike Isaiah, or David, or even Christ, I don't cry, "My God, my God." I just cry. At these times of spiritual emptiness I lack faith, either because I have forgotten the attachment or because it was never firmly established in the first place.

As the babies settle into their new home, small miracles occur. They grow. They get noisy and messy, active and curious. As they drink in the love and care that is given so freely, they come to believe in it, to want it, and finally, to expect and demand it. Despite the extra toll it puts on a staff member who has only two hands and one lap, new cries of protest at being placed in the playpen are met with great pleasure. The baby who once preferred to sit quiet and alone in an infant seat now makes absolutely sure that she gets *her* time in *those* arms in *that* rocking chair. The babies begin to move and explore. They crawl and stand. They take those early uncertain baby steps, and then, they are off and running. These are the signs of attachment, soon to be followed by all those entitled and glorious baby behaviors that say, "Look at me. Pay attention to me. Am I not wonderful?" Everyone and everything become "mine."

At rare times in my life, my relationship with God has been like that. When I called God "mine." When I was in close communication, making unlimited claims, requests, even complaints, confident that I would be heard.

There have been times when, even in my worst distress, I felt connected. I could call out, "My God, my God." It didn't matter what I said next. I could have been praising, bitching, or begging, but the foundation of a relationship was there. I had faith and felt the gift of comfort that comes with it.

But I see myself most clearly in the faces of the women who care for the babies. Beneath their smiles, I see their concerns. There are the anxieties about buffering these stigmatized children against a frightened world. There are concerns about keeping the house going in the midst of budget cuts and rising costs. And then there are the most difficult concerns of all—the knowledge that while some of these babies will convert to HIV-negative status over time, others will develop full-blown AIDS. And it isn't clear at the outset who will do which.

These are deeply spiritual women, and I marvel at their ability to do this work. How do they keep their faith in a God who allows all of this to happen? How do they go from a broken connection to one sweet child, to the loving care of another, knowing that the new baby will need the best they've got, but also knowing that they may get hurt again?

In situations like these, I have a very hard time with Jesus' instructions to just "consider the lilies of the field, how they neither toil nor spin." It's one of those teachings that is beautiful to hear and feels ridiculous to try to live. I spend at least three-quarters of my life toiling and spinning. I thought that was the whole point. I dismiss Jesus' words as poetic rhetoric. Easy for him to say, I think to myself. He's related to God. If my connections were that good, I'd cut down on the toiling and spinning, too.

Martha Manning

But I have more difficulty with the question he put to his disciples, "Can any of you by worrying add a single hour to your span of life?" It's a good question, and my answer is a wistful no. Otherwise, I would have accumulated at least three hundred years by now. But how else are we supposed to take care of the business of our lives, not to mention helping other people with theirs?

I trust worry more than I trust faith. Worry has so much evidence behind it; faith has so little.

Too often, I feel the erosion of faith in a God I want so badly to trust but somehow can't. Faith in God exists so easily for me in the light times, when it seems that God and I are of one mind about how my life should be going. But when things start going bad, my faith fades quickly into the growing shadows. I become like the young child who falls and hurts herself and then lashes out at her mother, assuming that since her mother was close by, she must have had some role in the pain, or at least some ability to stop it. I get stuck in my anger, paralyzed by a sense of betrayal and hopeless about the possibility of movement.

Faith is not a state into which I cross the border and establish permanent residence. No, I constantly move in and out of states of emptiness and detachment, innocent abandon and exhilaration, and attempts to reconcile an unjust and vicious world with a loving God. I wish I could just settle down with faith. I've come close but never lasted too long. The words of the poet Wendell Berry are a comfort to me in my frustration.

> We are fallen like the trees, our peace
> Broken, and so we must
> Love where we cannot trust,
> Trust where we cannot know.

I love those lines. They remind me that a spiritual journey is, in its *essence*, wavering and uncertain. But that's all right. Because the most important part of learning how to stand may be learning how to take a fall.

❧ SICK

THE THERMOMETER registered 103, and I felt every tenth of a degree past normal.

Not an inch of me was spared from sickness. Even my earlobes hurt. The chills took their turns with the sweats. My joints were so sore that it hurt to turn over in bed. And most alarmingly, my lungs were filling up by the minute. I called my friend Laura, a physician on the teaching faculty of a local university hospital, hoping that maybe she could stop by on her way home from work.

When I described my symptoms to her, she insisted that I come to the hospital because I might need X rays and a strong shot of antibiotics. She told me that it was her afternoon to supervise the residents in the outpatient clinic, so I'd have to go there to meet her. "Just tell them who you are," she instructed, "and someone will page me."

I struggled out of bed. I had just weathered a siege of shaking chills, so I was dressed in two pairs of ragged sweatpants, an unmatched pair of my husband's athletic socks, and a cast-off, putrid-yellow turtleneck that I had rescued years before from my father's giveaway pile. Completing the ensemble was a ripped and slightly filthy hooded sweatshirt. Whole sections of my hair asserted their independence from others, giving me the look of someone who has just inserted her hand into a live electrical outlet.

In my feverish state, I groped around for my keys, totally forgetting my purse, and shuffled out to my car, taking the tiny uncertain steps of someone at least fifty years older. Some people bear illness with a certain strength and nobility. I, on the other hand, just get really pathetic. I was, as we say in my house, "one hurtin' buckeroo." The only thing that reassured me was the knowledge that one of my best friends was twenty minutes away, willing and able to take good care of me and make me better.

It wasn't until I hit the parking garage and the attendant wanted money up front that I realized I was without money or identification. I swore to him that if he let me in, I'd borrow money from my friend—*who was a doctor*—and I'd give it to him on the way out.

He looked at me skeptically and called over the manager, who made me repeat the whole sad story. My silver, late-model Volvo station wagon—a veritable symbol of a certain level of income and status—was what I think finally convinced him to let me through.

Housed in the oldest section of the hospital, the outpatient clinic was a thoroughly dreary place, crammed with people slumped in plastic 1950s-looking chairs.

A ten-second survey of the waiting patients told me that if I wasn't sick coming in, I would definitely be sick going out. The air was thick with body odor, booze, and antiseptic. A raised glass fortress of a reception desk loomed in front of me.

I felt like Dorothy knocking on the door of the Great Oz. Three receptionists sat in swivel chairs. The expressions on their faces ranged from indifference to insolence.

The meanest of them grudgingly slid back the glass partition. Before I could get the first syllable out, she bellowed, "Did you sign in?"

"No, but—"

She thrust a clipboard at me and closed the glass. I signed my name and rapped again on the glass. With exaggerated effort she opened the window.

"I'm here to see Dr. Shelton," I told her with as much as-sertiveness as I could muster.

"Dr. Shelton isn't seeing patients today," she shot back.

"I'm Martha Manning. I'm a good friend of hers," I protested.

She looked me up and down, and it was obvious that she couldn't reconcile my appearance with my purported friendship with Dr. Shelton.

"Give me some I.D.," she demanded.

"I don't have any with me," I responded in disgrace.

She clucked with satisfaction, as if she had just cleverly ferreted out another impostor. "Sit down," she told me, "and wait your turn." She slammed the glass along its tracks and cut me off.

It was hard to find an empty seat in the crowded waiting room, since many of the people appeared to have brought along all their earthly possessions. No one made a move to clear a space for me. Finally, an elderly man cleared the seat next to him, placing his plastic bags on the floor by his feet.

"Miss," he called, "c'mon over here." I wasn't sure I wanted to go. But his toothless smile was the greatest act of kindness I had known all day, so I gratefully took the seat.

"You're not from here," he said knowingly. "What's ailin' you?"

"I don't know, but I'm really sick," I told him.

He felt my forehead and winced.

"Child, you be burnin' up," he told me. "And that cough is mean. Hope you don't have the TB," he added ominously.

"I think I've had a shot for that," I answered, hoping like hell that I was right.

"Then it have to be pneumonia," he pronounced with grave certainty. "Don't worry, they'll fix you up, give you shots and those big pills, and you'll be fine."

I was so grateful for his attention and confidence that I felt myself choking back tears.

Attempting to return the courtesy, I asked him what he was "in for."

Before I could stop him, he pulled off one shoe and two torn socks and showed me the worst-looking foot I have ever seen. I stifled a wave of nausea. He pointed out the various insults to his foot like a tour director, providing the history of every blister, bunion, lost nail, and possibly gangrenous toe. "Feets from the streets!" he said, grinning.

"How long do you usually have to wait to see a doctor in this place?" I asked.

"Two, three, maybe four."

"Hours?" I exclaimed.

"Yeah, girl," he chuckled, "no way you are from around here."

I started to cry, right there, right out loud. He bunched up a ratty wool blanket and placed it between my head and the wall.

"Just try to sleep," he told me. "It makes the time move faster."

I leaned back and closed my eyes. Occasionally I would open them to monitor the excruciatingly slow progress of the hands on the clock in front of me. My friend read old *National Geographics* and AAA driving-club magazines. I couldn't even read, which didn't matter much, since I was pretty sure that I was just going to die there.

After an hour, my next-chair-friend nudged me with his elbow. "Wake up, I think someone's lookin' for you." My friend Laura was behind the glass partition, looking very angry and blasting the receptionists. One of them got out of her chair and walked around into the waiting room.

"Dr. Manning," she said with exaggerated apology, "I am *so* sorry. Come right on back. You should have told us who you were."

In my head I screamed, *I'm the same poor sick slob I was an hour ago. Nothing about me has changed except your knowledge of my friendship with your boss and some fancy initials after my name.*

This interaction attracted a good deal of attention from the other waiting patients. As the receptionist motioned to lead me back to the examining room, clearly jumping me ahead of others who had been waiting longer, I felt caught right between the poor and the privileged. But I made no complaint. I handed the blanket back to the man next to me and wished him good luck with his feet. He returned the wish, winked at me, and predicted, "I'm bettin' on the pneumonia."

As I disappeared behind the glass, I was met with more apologies, combined with the same protestations, "If only we had known who you were." I was sick and groggy. Limp and weak. I didn't know the day or the time. Hell, by that point, I barely knew my own name.

The people in charge didn't know who I was. But the man sitting next to me knew. Without any credentials, he knew that I was sick and lost and scared. Did anything else matter?

❧ BUT FOR THE GRACE OF GOD

I PASSED A WOMAN sitting on the sidewalk last week. She was curled into herself like a snail in a shell. The area was full of homeless people, many of them greeting the morning with renewed energy for begging money and delivering proclamations to no one in particular. This woman didn't look like she'd been homeless for long. Her face lacked the color and lines that life on the street puts on a face, adding years with every month. Her stringy blonde hair hung dirty around her face, with roots that suggested several months since a dye job. She wasn't hanging out with anybody. She was just there. Alone. The way she looked and the way she held her body, or the way her body managed to hold her, portrayed a woman so locked in a private hell that her public hell on the streets looked like nothing in comparison.

My heart started picking up speed when I saw her. She made me sweat. At first I didn't know why. The "homeless mentally ill," as they are called, don't frighten me as much as they used to. People usually have interesting stories and opinions, even when some of the content or delivery of those stories sounds "crazy." But this woman didn't look crazy in that way. She looked like she was one step away from dead. Not physically dead—she was probably years away from that, unless she found the means to actively intervene sooner. The woman was soul-dead, self-dead. And she scared the hell out of me.

I too have been soul-dead and self-dead. So bad that I wanted to check out of my three-bedroom-brick-colonial, silver-Volvo, husband-and-daughter, loving-family-and-friends kind of life. Pretty crazy. So bad that I enhanced the profit margin of almost every major pharmaceutical company in the country searching for the cure. So bad that I ended up on a psychiatric unit. So bad that I asked to have an electrical current run through my brain in a last-ditch effort to find relief. I got a jump start before I completely and permanently stalled out. It worked.

I wrote a book. And then I toured the country talking about it. People seemed to like it. I've been praised for my courage. I have been thanked by hundreds of people for offering hope that they too might find their way out of the dark corners into which depression has trapped them. I read my book aloud as if it were a story with a beginning, a middle, and an end. The problem is that my life is not that story. In my life, I am in the *middle* of all of this, not at the end.

Mine is not a story of triumph where the protagonist prevails and there is an infinitely happy ending. There are periodical happy endings for me, punctuated by dark passages and frightening diversions. I have talked and written about depression with authority and passion. But I have not yet been able to do the thing that I most want to do with depression—defeat it, banish it, erect one nasty fence around me with a warning sign that promises I will shoot to kill should it ever haunt my premises again. The thing I want most is the thing I can't have.

It is hard to be a beacon of hope when despair still occupies one floor of my house. I'm not complaining. It used to have the run of the place. I have learned a couple of tricks that, for the time being, keep it contained. But when I talk to people about depression, I feel at times like the priest overcome with lust who tells the penitent to pray to God for self-control. I am the cop with blood on his hands telling a concerned citizen to trust in the system.

I see the woman on the street and think to myself, *There but for the grace of God go I.* On the surface, it is a humble statement, professing belief that the only reason I am upright and look functional at the moment is because of God's grace. The grace that spares me from a life on the streets includes money and health insurance, a strong net of people around me, good medical care, and a rainbow of pills. My last, most severe experience of depression taught me that without those gifts, I too could be hunched over on a street corner, looking closer to death than life.

But when I think hard about the statement "There but for the grace of God go I," I find no comfort. Because if I've learned anything from scripture, I've learned that what the Lord giveth, the Lord can sure as hell take away. And that scares the shit out of me. What is the difference between that woman and me? What is the difference, *within myself,* between that which is whole and that which is so badly broken? At best, they strike a tenuous balance inside me. When I begin to feel myself slip, and know that I am more broken than whole, I have trouble assuming the grace of God. Instead, I panic, convinced that *this* time I will be at the end of the line. This time, the very last bit of God's grace will go to the person in front of me, and I will be turned away empty. And then the sentence "There but for the grace of God go I" will become the unbearable "There . . . go I."

✣ CHASING GRACE

I WISH THERE WERE an installment plan for grace. So I would know that I was definitely going to get my monthly allotment—no matter what. But it never works like that. I'm never clear on whether it's *grace* that comes and goes, or whether it's my ability to *experience* it that varies so much. It seems like I'm always tearing after it, afraid I'll never catch it, or if I do, that there won't be enough.

I believe there are grace-filled people and places that are endowed with a spirit that pulls us toward them. In proximity to them, we feel different than we did before. Hope makes inroads into despair, forgiveness challenges anger, courage prevails over fear, and health conquers illness. People flock to the places where the Blessed Virgin has appeared in the form of weeping statues or healing wells, from Medjagorie to Lourdes to Conyers, Georgia. Her messages for the past years are so similar that they almost look trite printed on holy cards and medals. Work and pray for peace, she tells a world that finds it easier to believe in almost anything than the possibility of world peace.

I don't pretend to understand these things. I'm not even sure I believe in the actual fact of them. Does the statue cry real tears? Is Mary appearing in Georgia?

I don't know.

It doesn't really matter. Because I believe in the belief. When people gather to experience the power of that belief, I believe it is miraculous. I don't need to wait for the years of study and documentation by physicians and Vatican hotshots. I believe that when people sincerely seek holiness, they actually carry some of it with them to the destination of their pilgrimage. Their holiness combines with other people's holiness and the place becomes more sacred with time. Some would say it was sacred before the people started coming. That could be. But to me the greatest miracle is just that people come, and keep coming, to search, to worship, or just to hope.

When people take their sickness and suffering to hospitals, courts, and other human institutions, they are saying, "Here, use everything in your knowledge and technology to control this problem." Pilgrims come to holy places often having exhausted all those means of "control." They bring their broken selves, and in traveling to these shrines or trees or walls or wells, they acknowledge that ultimately they have no control, and they pray to their holy ones for mercy and healing. Sometimes they get the textbook cases of healing, the crutches thrown away, the sight restored, the cancer remitted.

Most of the time they get plain old mercy. Even if they still can't walk, or see, or show a clean X ray, there is a healing for their spirits. Nothing razzle-dazzle, no oh-my-God-it's-a-miracle! kind of stuff, but maybe just the energy to push on, the bolstering of a wavering faith, the reinforcement of hope, and the reminder that there is something greater than all of us, and that maybe, please God, there is a plan. Hopefully a *good* plan.

My holy place is a monastery. I go there to remember who I am. Sometimes I like the answer. Sometimes I don't. If there was ever a place of grace for me, it is that one, surrounded by the Blue Ridge Mountains and intersected by the Shenandoah River. Its holiness is in its simplicity, in its great reverence for nature and all other gifts of God. It is in Brother Stephen prefacing grace before the noontime meal with a description of three fledgling mockingbirds that ventured off the kitchen ledge earlier that morning. He describes the way they flew diagonally, where they flew, how their mother had to give them the tiniest push to leave, and how she's been squawking for over an hour because Stephen's cat, Buster, is on the porch, with her baby birds in plain sight.

This is not a polished act. Stephen talks about the birds haltingly, almost meditating on each just-spoken sentence. As we stand there waiting for lunch, I smile as he makes his first observation. Isn't that sweet . . . and profound, I think to myself. But that thought is immediately replaced with, Okay, let's cut to the chase, say grace, and eat. But then Stephen says the next sentence. And my head says, Okay, Stephen, you made your point. It's a miracle of nature. Let's get the show on the road. Then comes another sentence, a pause, and another sentence after that. Somewhere in there, my restlessness dissolves. I accept his rhythm in place of my own. I join him in trying to imagine what it is like for the mother to push the babies out of the nest, and how she feels right now, with Buster licking his chops down there. Stephen always ends his reveries with some slight self-deprecating remark about going off on tangents—but then he smiles in the smallest way and adds that *maybe* someone found *something* in it. I know that at least one person did, and say a silent amen. Stephen asks one of the nuns to say the grace. And I smile, knowing I just said mine.

The repetition of the monastery invites me to slow down, which is so hard for me to do. Some of the services that mark the monks' days allow for slight variations in content. Others are exactly the same *every single day.* Chants, readings, and prayers. The same time, the same words, the same hypnotic melody. On the first day of every retreat, I can't wait for the services. They move me so much that I become quite convinced that I am an excellent candidate for the monastic life. But by the second day I squirm in my seat and my clothes feel uncomfortable as I endure the long chanted prayers. Didn't we just do this *yesterday?* I think impatiently. How do these guys stand it? Does anyone just go wild one day and break out singing "I Can't Get No Satisfaction" or "Losing My Religion"? I can almost feel the remote control in my hand, flicking it with itchy fingers, desperate for something to engage my hard-to-hold attention.

When I return to my room, my eyes sweep the space, instinctively checking for faxes, mail, and messages. I pace the room for a while, think about how long before it will be all right to grab another piece of cake from the dining room, and figure out how the hell I am going to kill the three hours till bedtime. I wonder how I've ever lasted five days before—no talking, no business, no television or radio. No nothing.

And then something happens. I remember why I am at a monastery and not a hotel. Hotels don't have monks. So I watch the monks. And in watching them I realize what I have lost and come to understand how I might get it back. I remember how to look closer and longer, to listen harder, to recover that fragile sensuality that is so easily snuffed out by the sensory overkill in my life. I find joy, where it's always been, in the broad brush-strokes of the mountains, when their color changes from green to blue as day moves toward night. It is in the details. The joy is in finding the best corner of the meditation chapel to watch the sunset, the many differences in the songs of the birds, the walk in darkness from the chapel to the guest house, my steps crunching on the gravel, guided by the narrow cast of my flashlight in a mist so thick I imagine, for a moment, that it's heaven.

At the monastery, everything becomes a prayer. Reading. Walking. Even washing the dishes. When I maximize any experience by appreciating the richness of its simplicity, I come closer to the holiness I so desperately seek. It is here that I stop chasing grace like it's a subway car just closing its doors. At the monastery, I stop all the running, and finally, I let grace find its way to me.

❧ BARBIE

AT THE AGE OF EIGHT I knew Barbie better than I knew my father. I adored her. She was so much better than the clunky life-sized Patty Play Pal and the baby dolls that cried and wet. Somehow they didn't project me into fantasies about any kind of exciting future. Barbie was a doll, but she was also a dream. A perfect woman with a perfect (albeit anatomically incorrect) man. In Barbie's early days, there was only one doll with an ever-expanding wardrobe. I had each and every outfit and its accessories memorized from the Barbie preview brochures at the toy store.

My father's ignorance of Barbie was surpassed only by my mother's disapproval of her. She reluctantly allowed me to buy one *with my own money,* but no way was she ever letting Ken in the house. My mother said that "real women" were not like Barbie, as if that were some kind of revelation. Real women weren't like Snow White, Cinderella, and Rapunzel either, but no one seemed to care. Besides, I was an eight-year-old girl who basically didn't give a damn about "real women," whoever they were.

I spent hours lost in fantasy with Barbie. She wasn't just a doll to dress up in flashy outfits, impossibly arched, tiny high heels, and smart accessories. I didn't just want to *have* Barbie. I wanted to *be* her. I give my mother credit for allowing me to have a doll with that much power. But I think that she had faith that ultimately I would figure out the Big Barbie Lie on my own. She was right. My developing body didn't look a bit like Barbie's, and it was becoming pretty clear that it never would. It wasn't just the doll I rejected. It was the persona. Barbie was the illusion of perfection for a woman. Barbie never had to deal with acne and stringy hair. There was no such thing as "Bad Cramps" Barbie. Barbie was always snagging the hot guys just by being pretty and wearing great clothes and saying absolutely nothing, an accomplishment I knew was considerably more complicated than that. There was no "How to Behave with Boys" Barbie, in which half of her brain was detachable for dates. Over time, the intensity of my love for her turned to hate. Barbie was the biggest lie perpetrated on girls. I swore that if I ever had a daughter, she would never, ever have a Barbie.

My daughter started asking for Barbie when she was two years old. I held out until she was three. I bought her one, but then constantly injected lines like "You know, no woman looks like that; it's physically impossible" as she was playing. My feminist comments were met with a "Yeah, sure . . ." dismissal or "Mom, when can I get Pretty-in-Pink Barbie?" Fortunately, my daughter left Barbie in much the same way I did. Now in adolescence, she has nothing but contempt for Barbie and the message to girls that she represents. Actually, the only person in my very large family who really likes Barbie these days is my father.

When my father retired, he worked as an investigator for a Senate subcommittee and then as director of security for stores and foundations. After a number of years, he pronounced himself ready to "really" retire. Three weeks later, he couldn't stand being idle. My mother was totally immersed in her work every day, so he was on his own. He began taking on part-time jobs, as a sales representative for a feminine hygiene company, then an upscale skin-care company, and then a large candy conglomerate. The pay was lousy, but my father stayed busy. The added bonus of the jobs was that he got surplus or expired samples and products. There was something so humbling about my father opening the trunk of his Volvo, surveying his bounty, and asking if we were regular or super absorbency, or advising us not to take it personally as he handed us a bottle of antidandruff shampoo and asked if we had ever considered using it. Being allowed to pick out handfuls of our favorite candy was like being kids again, especially as we reverted to type when the demand outstretched the supply and it was every sibling for him- or herself.

Now past seventy, my father has given up those jobs. He volunteers his time picking up leftover food from stores and delivering it to homeless shelters and soup kitchens. He also collects Barbies.

While accompanying my mother to a craft show where she was exhibiting, he noticed the brisk sales at the next booth. He approached the woman at the booth and learned that Barbie is big business. People pay major money for these dolls. Immediately, he decided to become a dealer. My father never wades toe-by-toe into new water. He jumps right in. At times, this has created some problems in my family, like when I casually wished I had a horse and all of a sudden we had a Shetland pony in the back of our station wagon.

But Barbie has turned out to be a good bet. He has at least eight hundred of them, all untouched in their perfect pink boxes. They are stacked under every bed, in closets and corners. He has them inventoried on his computer. He belongs to all the Barbie collector clubs and contributes to the Barbie newsletter. He juggles these activities with planning his Marine Corps reunion activities. He couldn't give one damn about the inconsistencies among his appearance, his history, and his current interests. He can quote the market value on any limited-edition Barbie and has been very successful at turning a profit. "I'm not in love with Barbie," he insists. "I think she's a mess. No girl could look like that. If she didn't have good clothes, she'd be down the drain."

He's got us all in on the act now. He faxes my brothers, sisters, and me about calling stores and catalogs with new special-order Barbies when there is a limit on the number that may be purchased. I'll walk into my study at 6:00 A.M. and there will be a fax from my father: "KIDS CALL NOW—Macy's Winter Princess Barbie. Two to a person. Price is . . . Product number . . . They're extremely limited, so do it FAST. Pay you back. Love, DAD."

He has us so well trained that none of us can pass a Barbie aisle without searching for "finds." I have called him from toy stores, sitting on the floor with my cellular phone in one hand and a Barbie box in the other. Mothers and their daughters step over me and puzzle over my half of our conversations, "No, she looks intact. . . . She's cheap. . . . Why do you think she's a loser?"

Recently I carried ten limited-edition dolls to the cashier of a major retail store. I struggled with the stack of ten boxes in the long line. When my turn came, I gingerly placed each box on the belt and after she rang each one up, I took it back and packed it myself. (Barbie values plummet if she or her box looks like used goods.) As we were waiting for that special cash-register noise that reassures me that I still have some credit left, the cashier beamed at me and exclaimed,

"You are going to make a lot of little girls mighty happy!"

"Well, actually," I told her, "they're for my father."

She and I realized instantly that I had just made my father sound like a pervert. It was clear that neither of us wanted to pursue any exploration of the issue.

In the car with my ten virgin, undented Barbies, I laughed to myself at the silliness of a forty-three-year-old woman buying ten Barbies for her father. But then I laughed at myself. For too long, I believed that the self I chose to be would be set in concrete by my thirties. I was just meant to live it all out to its conclusion after that. But I see how my mother evolved in her forties—from the traditional duties of homemaking to painting and sculpting, casting, making paper, relishing the challenge of the best ways to combine a feather found on a walk, a jagged stone from a grandchild, and a piece of fabric from an old dress into something interesting and beautiful, even if only to her.

I see my proud young father in photographs from the Marines, then all decked out in his black cassock, one step away from the priesthood. I see him in a suit, a badge, and a gun. I see him running the Boston Marathon at the age of fifty, doing one leg of the twenty-six miles with a priest who heard his confession and prayed the rosary with him. I see him on his bike and playing pickup hockey. I see him with the guys.

But now, I also see him as the one who bakes each of our birthday cakes—always dense pound cake with white frosting and our names written in script. I see him shopping and sharing the cooking with my mother. I see him writing and sending out bulletins and newsletters about our family. I see him wearing tennis shorts in the winter, walking as fast and hard as anyone I know. I see him get pissed off as easily and apologize as quickly as he ever did. I see him as a man who has lost his church, but not his religion. And I see him with Barbie. Somehow, it all fits.

My parents remind me that the cement may get poured, but that doesn't mean it has to set.

❧ I TAKE IT ALL BACK

AS KIDS IN CATHOLIC SCHOOL we always prayed for "vocations." A vocation was much more than a job, or even a career. A "true" vocation involved becoming a nun or a priest. Even the vocations of spouse and parent were distant seconds to "answering the call." The response to the constant question, "How do I know if I *have* a vocation?" always came with an ethereal, knowing smile and the words, "You just know. You hear God's call. You can't miss it."

Before the age of eleven, I wanted with all my heart to become a nun. I was fascinated by the way they moved in their long black robes with countless folds, with sleeves that went on forever and from which they pulled the most extraordinary things—tissues, old cough drops, even an eraser or a ruler every now and then. Their long, almost floor-touching rosary beads swung like pendulums as they paced the aisles of their classroom kingdoms. I was intrigued by the high, black, noiseless shoes that helped them sneak up behind children and magically catch them in some act of misbehavior.

I loved watching them walk from the convent to the church across the blacktop to 7:00 A.M. daily mass. On a winter day, with their heads bent into the wind and their long black capes trailing, they looked holier than priests. I was convinced that their vocation as nuns brought them supernatural powers that bypassed most priests. Those women had the ability to see behind them, the capacity to chuck an eraser across the room to smack the head of an unruly boy, so that all of us straightened up before the chalk dust had fully settled on his head. Watching the finesse with which a nun could force a confession of classroom crime, following a grilling that made the guys on *Dragnet* look complacent, I often found myself simultaneously admiring her skill and hating her for it.

Even as a young girl I knew that some of these women were nuns by default. Their meanness, while inflicted upon us, was not caused by us. They probably joined the convent because no one else would have them. But there were other nuns. They were tall and graceful—women you believed could actually have had real lives before this. They were smart and strong—forceful without being cruel. They were our models of women without men. The deference they taught us to adopt the moment that "Father" walked into the room was nothing compared with the welcome we were to give Sister Mary Principal when she walked in. I admired these women. I wanted to become them.

I practiced being a nun, putting my hands up my bathrobe sleeves, taking the brass ring off the top of the standing lamp in my room and securing it over an old slip for a veil. I paced up and down my room as if it had rows of desks. I read the lives of the saints—particularly the virgin martyrs. Then I narrowed it down to just the virgins because that seemed like the easiest way to get into heaven. You didn't have to keep your virginity *and* boil in oil. You just had to keep your virginity. Whatever that was.

I informed my parents quite piously, as if I were delivering a message from God, that I had "a vocation." I don't know exactly what I expected from them, but I thought it would involve tears of joy and a great deal of praise. I definitely didn't expect my mother to sigh and reach into the refrigerator for a jar of mustard or for my father to smirk and continue carving the ham. I began to identify with all those poor young saints I had read about.

"Did you hear what I said? I have a vocation," I repeated.

"That's lovely, dear," my mother said without even looking up from her cooking, "but give it some time. You may change your mind."

She and my father exchanged one of those infuriatingly private looks that are the parent equivalent of children's secret handshakes. This must be just how Saint Bernadette and Saint Teresa "the Little Flower" felt. Just as they did, I steeled myself, "I will consider this the first test of my convictions." I would be relentless in enlightening them.

I became publicly pious. While my family sat in the den watching TV, reading, playing games, and engaging in the usual jousting and bickering, I entered the room in silence, my sanctimonious head held high, always wearing a long robe with my rosaries in my pocket. I would hold the family Bible and sit erect and totally uncomfortable in full view of everyone, reading the scriptures or praying the rosary silently while they diddled away time in their worldly pedestrian pursuits. I prayed for their souls, particularly for my parents—devout Catholics who had just strayed in this particular instance. I prayed for God to convince them that I was one of the "chosen" but vowed that even without their enlightenment, I would walk a road so holy that they could not possibly create detours.

But instead of enlightening my parents, God chose to enlighten me. Not with visions, or even voices. Just hormones. Sexuality replaced piety in my thoughts and my goals. I developed intense and simultaneous crushes on several boys, each of whom returned the favor. The boys that, years before, I had scorned on the playground became the sole focus of my attention. One day when David Reardon's starched white school shirt brushed against mine and he let it just stay there for probably three whole seconds, I realized that heaven was no farther away than the seat next to me. And I realized that I was destined for love.

Then it hit me. Just as in those fables and fairy tales in which the wishers realize that they've been wishing for something they absolutely didn't want, there I was up against a lifetime of wishing, and even praying, for God to give me a vocation.

How do you tell God you've changed your mind? Is wishing and praying a scorecard deal—if you have a backlog of prayers for one thing and then you change your mind, can you wipe the slate clean and start over? If it happens with sin, it most surely happens with prayers, I reassured myself. I was confused about the technicalities here, but there was one thing about which I was totally sure. No way was I ever going to be a nun.

The nuns knew about these things. For the budding adolescent girl they had a second-line offense, which was basically the philosophy of "It's too late now, honey. Your draft notice is already in the mail." They began to tell us stories about an anonymous young girl—always the most popular in school, the one liked best by all the girls and boys. The girl's life is one constant date. Every boy loves her. The nuns really built her up so we would totally identify with her. They continued these stories, to which we were by then addicted, enumerating the many ways in which the girl retained her chastity/honor/modesty/self-respect or any other euphemism for not letting a boy put his filthy hands on her. And in the midst of this whirl of social life to which we all aspired, suddenly it hits her like a flying object: A VOCATION. In one instant she knows that she will be a nun. She immediately renounces the trivialities of her former life, and (the nuns were really smart here) against the wishes of her family and friends who wanted her to have an "ordinary life," she enters a convent immediately following her high-school graduation.

This was a truly effective campaign, because it emphasized the fact that you had absolutely no idea what you were up against. If it could happen to the homecoming queen, it could happen to you. You could really like boys and still be ejected from the game.

I began to understand the true meaning of this "chastity" that I had always heard about but had never fully comprehended as a child. Because the nuns always emphasized the concept of "purity" and linked it somehow to men, I figured it was no big deal. Until recently, I hadn't considered males as anything more than a nuisance, making chastity a breeze. The vows of obedience and poverty seemed clearly the most difficult. If you didn't know what the "marital act" was, how could you miss it?

But with the onset of puberty, chastity immediately became the most difficult. Poverty began to look better and better. I decided that I would live in a tent to be with Timothy Gavigan. I would survive on bread and water if I could kiss Anthony Gallo. Even in the obedience department I knew I wasn't giving my full effort to my parents, and vowed to improve. But this chastity thing no longer felt like it was under my control. I still adored my virgin martyrs, but I began to think that maybe their being martyrs had something to do with the fact that they were virgins. It was like they surrendered their tickets before they'd seen the show.

I was a poor wretch of a twelve-year-old whose sexuality was flooding her system and overloading her circuits. And all I cared about was having my years of vocation prayers reversed, undone, or whatever it took to make them totally null and void. I became paranoid, wondering if the nuns targeted particular girls—as in the football draft, where coaches surveyed the players and chose the best draft picks. It was like reverse voodoo. You were targeted for something they thought was great but you thought was horrible.

Each time we bowed our heads and prayed to God that we would be "blessed" with the "gift" of a vocation, I held my own private desperate conversation with God. *Please God, not me. I've changed my mind. Totally. I take it all back.* Then I'd aim my eyes and prayers at Bernadette Meehan, front-runner for May Queen because her mother sucked up to the nuns by driving them all over the place. *Pick her,* I would pray. *She's smart. She's ugly. And she hates boys. She's perfect. Choose her, but please God, not me.* I'd close my eyes tight to ward off any prayers that were headed in my direction, like the way we'd scrunch down in the hallways with our coats over our heads for disaster drills just in case The Communists dropped a bomb on our school. Even as a little kid, I knew that techniques like that were in the kiss-your-ass-good-bye realm of protection, but I'd do them anyway—on the infinitesimal chance that they might save me.

But I wasn't taking any chances. I would do everything I could to be declared 4–F in this particular battle for my soul. I would test chastity even if it meant that I would, for all eternity, lose out on the possibility of ever becoming a virgin martyr, or even May Queen. Through my own battle with chastity I would ensure that anything in the vocation arsenal being aimed my way would bounce off me as if I were Teflon. I would do anything to be safe. Impure, yes; immodest, yes; in mortal sin, yes—but heart-racingly and heartbreakingly delivered from the dismal prospect of a life of sainthood.

❧ HEAVEN

I WAS NOT a good infant mother. Partly because my daughter was not a good infant. From the moment my water broke, nothing turned out as I had expected. I did everything within my power to have a natural childbirth. She did absolutely nothing to help.

There's nothing like twenty-four hours with labor-inducing drugs followed by a C-section to make you wonder what was ever meant by "natural." Top that off with a terrible infection; veins that kept collapsing, necessitating ten days of traveling IVs; a Foley catheter; a vertical scar that began at my belly button and didn't seem to end; and antibiotics so thick that nurses held the shots behind their backs and it felt like I was being injected with knitting needles.

My daughter was beautiful, partly because she was just an attractive child, but mostly because she didn't have to push her way out of her comfortable home. She gave the slightest signal and, twenty-four hours later, I was cut open and she was gently lifted out. Given the ease of her arrival, I anticipated a bit more cooperation in the few things I expected of her—like eating and sleeping. But she was a lousy eater and a worse sleeper. When my milk came in, I felt like I had hot rocks on my chest, and I really could have used her cooperation. But she wasn't interested in what I had to offer. I had carefully read the La Leche League books and pamphlets and was looking forward to breast-feeding. Some women actually had orgasms while breast-feeding. But I had to have nurses come in to "teach" me how to breast-feed, something I'd seen cats and dogs accomplish without a bit of instruction. When it became clear that I was ill, they suggested that it might be better to give up the idea of breast-feeding and put her on the bottle instead.

But after the entire childbirth fiasco, I was goddamned if I was going to forgo my last shot at natural. My fever was 104. Everything around me felt like one of those mirages you see in shots of the desert, where in the blinding sunlight everything seems to glimmer and shake. All I remember from that time is voices, and a big milking machine on wheels. They hooked me up, pulled the switch, and let 'er rip. The relief I felt rivaled the very worst time I had to pee. But as grateful as I was, I also felt like my name should be "Bessie" and I belonged in Farmer John's barn. The machine made incredible noise. It felt like it could suck even the breath out of me. People came in and out of my room as casually as if I were eating breakfast. Almost every orifice I had was either leaking or had something on it or in it. It was the *least* natural time of my entire life.

I often wonder if that was the reason Keara and I got off to a slow start. Even when she finally took to the breast, she was what the pediatrician called a "nibbler," meaning she'd take a few slugs and go to sleep for twenty minutes, only to wake up and want to do the whole thing again. I had a friend whose baby was classified as a "barracuda." She'd feed ravenously and fall into a drunken stupor for at least four hours. Keara didn't sleep for four straight hours until she was eight months old.

She also had colic, which in the late seventies meant that I was doing something very wrong. After the usual offending foods were excluded, I became the primary suspect. I must be too "uptight," too "nervous," and I was communicating it to her. It was a good thing mothers aren't licensed. I wouldn't have gotten past my learner's permit. To have to deal with my baby's discomfort was hard enough. Feeling *responsible* for it was awful.

Keara never slept for more than two hours at a time at night and rarely slept at all during the day. I learned firsthand what I had studied in graduate school—the terrible effects that sleep deprivation can have on perfectly nice people. It didn't help being a psychologist-in-training. With each hostile feeling, with each failure, I mentally registered a setback in my baby's emotional development. The pediatrician tried to comfort me by saying that the brightest babies need the least amount of sleep. But I wasn't thinking of Harvard at that point. I just wanted some rest.

I wished I could have found a way to stuff her back inside me for just a few more months. She and I had both been so much more comfortable with that arrangement. The expression "but the cat was out of the bag" held new meaning for me.

I loved my daughter. I really did. When she was sucking or sleeping, I stared at her with reverence, admiring the crown of her smooth head, her chubby cheeks, her graceful fingers. I loved the music of saying her name, rhyming it with other words into makeshift lullabies. In the rare quiet, I loved rocking her when her body was relaxed and loose. The problem was, when she wasn't eating or sleeping, she was the personification of misery. And I have to admit, at those times I didn't *like* her all that much.

It's a terrible feeling to think you are a bad mother and that you still have fifty or sixty years to go. No longer did I separate the days from the nights, the weekdays from the weekends. Life was one long wailing cry—hers and mine.

Over the next few months, we slowly warmed to each other. Taking care of her was still a totally absorbing experience. I charged at my husband as he unlocked the apartment door every day at 5:30 and passed her off with the speed of a great running back. I still thank God there were no sharp metal objects around when he would ask, "So what did you two do today?" or "How long has it been since you washed your hair?"

Keara and I began to make prolonged eye contact. There was a building anticipation in our bodies for each other. She kicked in her crib when she saw me coming, and I felt my heart beat faster in response. We molded to each other's curves. She ate a little more, slept a little more, and cried a little less. I started to wear real clothes during the day and sometimes had the energy to pull something out of the freezer and throw it into the oven. Her developmental milestones were on schedule. Maybe this was the best I could hope for.

We finally found a mutually agreeable way to spend our time. She loved it when I read to her. She didn't care what it was, as long as I read it with a high-pitched voice and frequent changes in inflection. I read my psychology journals aloud to her as if I were reading "Jack and Jill went up the hill . . ." The fact that I was quoting reliability coefficients and using words that only psychologists understand was no problem. At any pause she smiled, flailed her arms a little, and looked at me with a silent command to keep going. I started to smile again.

One morning, as I launched into a series of articles in search of a dissertation topic, Keara discovered her feet. She had noticed her hands weeks before and was beginning to find a variety of uses for them, from comforting herself by sucking on her fist to swiping at objects and grabbing them in an iron lock in her tenacious little fingers. But the feet were new. And so were those little things I put on her feet every day, heavier than socks, meant to keep babies' feet warm. With their elasticized band, they were also meant to stay on longer than regular socks.

Once babies discover their feet, they love to grab their toes. Removing a sock becomes a game. Keara played with her socks and I read. After a few minutes, she started gurgling and laughing. I looked up at her and saw that she held her little yellow sock in her hand. It was her first catch. A proud moment. She tilted her head a bit, looked straight at me with a "watch this" kind of expression, and placed the sock on her head. She sat there staring at me with the sock on her head and the goofiest expression on her face, waiting for me to respond. I laughed with more spontaneity and joy than I'd felt in months. She took the sock off her head. Then she gave me the look again and put it back on. I laughed so hard my ribs hurt. Tears cascaded down my face. Again and again, she took the sock off and then put it back on her little bald head. And every time, I laughed more than the time before. It was our first true moment of shared joy. It catapulted us from a relationship defined by milking, sleeping, and passing gas to one defined by the deepest knowledge and enjoyment of each other.

When my husband called that afternoon, I immediately burst out laughing. Keara was sitting in the infant seat beside me. Given my track record over the previous months, Brian thought I was sobbing.

"What's wrong?" he asked with alarm.

"Brian," I gulped, "Keara . . . *put a sock on her head!*"

"And?. . . " Brian asked while I laughed hysterically.

"Oh. . . . That's it. . . . It's just that she put this yellow sock on her head and it was . . . so unbelievably funny."

As if she knew what was happening, Keara put the sock on her head again.

"Oh my God . . . she's doing it again!" I cried. I couldn't contain myself.

"Well, that's good . . . I guess," said Brian tentatively. "Why don't we talk about it when I get home." He was probably mentally calculating whether we could afford for me to see a therapist.

I was laughing so hard I couldn't say good-bye.

I became Keara's mother that day. And she became my child. We made each other laugh, without words or fancy props, with just a sock and some goofy looks. It was a perfect moment—two people realizing their absolute resonance with each other. When I try to imagine what heaven is like, I think of that day. The joy that was born between us bubbled over into the next day, the next month, and the next year.

It is seventeen years later and I still laugh. Brian and Keara look at me strangely as I try to recount the story between gasps for laughter and air. One of them always complains, "Oh no, it's the sock story." I dismiss Brian because he wasn't even there. But I look to Keara, hoping to give her some cue that will shake loose those old preverbal memories, so that we can share the joy of that day—even though I know she was much too young to have the memory. They wait out my hilarity on the subject, which remains a solitary experience.

When I finally settle down, Keara teases me with the old line, "Guess you had to be there . . ."

And I always reply, "Oh, but you *were* there, baby. You really were."

❧ MARY

I NEVER FELT much affinity for Mary, the mother of Christ. So many of the other people in the Bible were more fleshed out, real to me in one way or another. They offered something with which I could identify or resonate. But Mary was a blank screen—formless and diffuse. Through her I received the Catholic church's formulation of the perfect woman. I had it hammered into me, year after year, that Mary was the model to which I should aspire: pure, passive, and docile.

None of these traits felt particularly salient in adolescence when I began to feel more akin to Mary, as in Magdalene, than to Mary, as in Blessed Virgin. Mary's most quoted line, "May it be done to me according to your word," was a foreign concept to me. I lived by the credo "Let *me* do it according to *my* word."

My indifference to Mary turned humorous by high school, when the nuns launched their all-out crusade for our purity. Somehow the program just didn't catch on with me. I never found myself fending off unduly passionate dates with the surefire phrase, "Is this the way you would treat our Blessed Mother?"—one of the many chastity zingers given by Sister Mary Jerome that were guaranteed to stop boys dead in their tracks *and* cause them to have the highest respect for us.

In the years following high school, as I became more involved in feminism, my bemusement with Mary turned to outright disdain.

Her supposed passivity irked me. All she seemed to do was endure everything—from having to explain with a straight face that she had been impregnated by God, to trying to keep up with her son, who was also God, to watching him work plenty of miracles but not enough to save himself from dying young. Her reaction to so many events was silence. She just "kept things in her heart." This woman seemed to offer nothing to me in the role-model department. In fact, she served as the antithesis of everything I hoped to become.

Mary remained irrelevant for years—until one afternoon in Bloomingdale's. I was shopping for a gift with my daughter, who had recently turned two. At that feisty age, she no longer felt any particular need to hang close to me. She chose, instead, to explore the wonders of the Juniors department. I bent over to inspect a price tag, and when I stood up she was gone. Not two aisles over. Gone.

I have answered frightening phone calls in the middle of the night. I have been in car wrecks. I have walked into my house while a burglary was in progress. But nothing compared with the screaming, helpless, paralyzed terror of having my daughter wander off in a huge, public place.

I ran down aisles, brushing against racks of clothes, frantically calling her name. A saleswoman searched the dressing room. Another alerted neighboring departments. What was probably only a period of four or five minutes expanded in that eternal way that fear has of simultaneously making time speed up and slow down.

As a saleswoman dialed the number for store security, I heard the faint sounds of my daughter's giggle. She was nowhere in sight, so I followed the laughter and found her sitting contentedly in the middle of a circular rack of full-length coats, totally hidden from view. When she spotted me, she whooped loudly and clapped her hands in delight, as if we had just played the most enjoyable game of hide-and-seek. All the desperation that had been caught in my throat now came out in tears as I hugged her close to me. She wriggled from my grasp, looking totally puzzled by my tears, and piped up, "Mommy . . . play again?"

Riding down the escalator with her tiny mittened hand in mine, I had a kind of biblical flashback. All of a sudden, I remembered the story of Mary losing Jesus for three whole days, searching for him frantically, only to eventually find him upstaging his elders in the temple. He was as oblivious to her distress as my daughter was to mine. I puzzled over Mary's reaction to what I considered a typical adolescent smart-ass response when she protested his disappearance. Jesus basically dismissed her by saying that he had bigger things to worry about. Somehow, in that department store, I had a bit more empathy for what it was like for Mary to experience something about her child that she could not totally understand or control. I realized that sometimes there is nothing else to do as a parent but reflect on those moments, as she did, and "hold them in your heart."

My two-year-old became fifteen. And in the intervening years, I found other opportunities to understand Mary. One Sunday morning at mass, the priest read yet another of the many drafts of the U.S. Bishops' pastoral letter on women, which insulted every Catholic woman by saying basically, "We think you're great. You can be in the club. But remember, you'll never learn the secret handshake." A man stood in the middle of the congregation at the church my husband and daughter attend. He stood there silently and prayerfully. But his standing caused a number of heads to turn. After the liturgy, my husband approached him about his reasons for standing. The man replied, "I can no longer sit with the sin of sexism." The next week several more people stood, among them my husband and daughter.

The fury that this unleashed in the parish was unanticipated in its intensity and depth. Angry meetings were held. Friendships and working relationships were threatened. The overwhelming majority opinion was clear: those standing should immediately sit down. Several people did. But my husband and daughter stood their ground.

My husband sang in the choir at the front of the church. My daughter stood by herself in the congregation, along with two or three other people throughout the church. She vowed to stand "until women are allowed to become priests." I warned her that her red hair could go gray before that happened. She was undeterred.

I taught my daughter all my lofty ideals with energy and righteousness. I taught her to stand up for her beliefs. I never knew that she would take me so literally. My daughter has opinions about everything, and she is absolutely unabashed in her willingness to share them. Even when I disagree with her, I admire the color that rises in her cheeks, the strength that grows in the volume of her voice, the emphasis of her strong hands, and the magic she works with words when she feels fierce and right.

Throughout the process at church, as I saw the deep anger and resentment engendered by just a couple of people choosing to remain vertical during mass, I became afraid. I realized that I had been generous with my daughter in the self-esteem department and stingy in teaching her the consequences of being that self. In a world where the collision between a strong-opinioned girl and a situation she finds untenable most resembles the combination of a lit match and gasoline, I know that it is the girl who will get burned.

When you stand up for your beliefs, it might not do any good. Moreover, bad things can happen. People will get mad at you. They may not like you. You may find yourself isolated. You may get yourself into trouble. Like many women, I've spent most of my life believing on some level that these are risks that should be avoided. It's taken me years to learn to tolerate the fact that when I exercise my authority, I may be called a bitch. My daughter does not assess the risks as I do. Despite my gentle cautions, she just doesn't seem to care. That is why I am afraid. That is why I think about Mary these days.

What must it have been like to be the mother of Jesus, watching him walk toward his destiny, even when she couldn't understand it? What must it have been like for her to watch him mature and make his place in the world as a teacher, a healer, a leader? She must have been so proud. But at the same time, what was it like to see that those very things that made her so proud were also engendering suspicion, envy, and hatred all around him? And what was it like to lose him for all those things that made him so special? Small comfort to know that it was his destiny—and hers.

Pride and fear live right next to each other in a parent's heart. Sometimes, what makes us most proud of our children is also what makes us most afraid. The mothers of martyrs know this all too well. I have done what I could to lay the groundwork as a parent. But what happens with it is, to a great extent, beyond my control.

As with all children, my child is meant to wander away from me, to places where I will be unable to protect her. I admire her principles and her tenacity, but I worry about the risks she will incur in their expression. So, like Mary, I pray for the patience to be able to let go. To be able to "reflect on things" and "hold them in my heart." But more than anything, I pray for a heart that is strong enough to bear them.

❧ TO BE DELIVERED

TODAY IS MY DUE DATE. It has been long in coming. Nine months to be exact. But there will be no baby. Not today. Not tomorrow. Not next week. The baby left months ago. But the due date remains. Despite all my attempts to face the facts, that day is as real to me now as it was when the doctor added up the numbers, turned the wheel, and noted where the arrow landed. Disregarding all evidence, I persist in the countdown.

Chasing Grace

The day was marked on the calendar in the kitchen. It said in my daughter's best hand, "BABY IS DUE." But now, despite the three different-colored crayons she used to block out that square, I can still see the words. All the other boxes have numbers and words that say where I'm headed. But this box—the blue-green-brown box—says where I've been.

I hold on to the due date with the tenacity of the calendar on the wall. When you lose a baby, it takes time for your body to understand. Everything in you has worked so hard to get that new life started. And then, suddenly, the effort is unnecessary.

But the news is slow in getting to the outposts. Your body is pregnant, without the baby. The nausea and fatigue that you tolerated in the name of paying your dues are now cruel reminders of the futility of the exercise.

Slowly, your body takes the hint. Your breasts and belly shrink. The nausea abates, and you climb back on the carousel to ride round and round again. But that is not the end. There are farther outposts still. Like the soldiers in wars who haven't heard the news and stand ready to fight long after their country has surrendered, a part of me hasn't caught on and hasn't given up.

I live in two realities. They run parallel, never touching or reconciling. I am a woman with one child who has lost another. That woman accepts what is real.

But I am also a woman with one child who is expecting another—anytime now.

That woman comes alive in dreams, where I rock beautiful babies with shining eyes and we hold wordless conversations that make us smile. It comes in moments when, drifting into waking, I wonder for a split second how I can still sleep on my stomach. It comes when I hear other women's due dates and automatically calculate how close we are in time.

That part of me is still counting and waiting. I refuse to acknowledge that at the end of this day I will have no more than I did yesterday. I don't surrender easily. Because in the surrender I must admit that it's over, really over. I did what I could and it wasn't enough. And I'm not sure I can bear it.

I can't bear the aching emptiness when I see an infant in the safe arms of its mother. I despise the frozen, self-conscious smile fixed on my face as I endure other women's pregnancy stories. I hate the people stopped in traffic when I see their babies unsafe and loose in their seats.

These two parts of me—the pregnant one and her empty companion—have come to the crossroads. Today our separate journeys must seek a single destination. It is time, not to surrender but to make peace. The empty one has to hold back the words *I told you so*, and the pregnant one must face her truth, understanding that she has lost her baby, but not herself. These two women must reconcile so that I can finally free myself from this painful past.

So good-bye, child. You let go of me. It's time I let go of you. It's time to free you from that place in me where you are frozen in time, broken and lost. We were not meant to live together in the light, but come to me in darkness. Visit me in dreams, sweet child, where you are whole and perfect, never hurting or hungry, and I am never sad. Play on, forever safe in my imagination, where you will always be the dream child, my perfect possibility.

Go on now. I have labored long enough. After all the time and all the pain, I am ready. To push on and out. To let go and take hold. Today is my due date.

And I am ready to be delivered.

❧ COLLEGE

THERE IS A NEW BOOKCASE in our dining room. Our house is already full of bookcases. But we always seem to need more. Like our cars, they all have names. There are bookcases called Religion, Poetry, Travel; several named Literature; several,

Psychology, Depression, Cooking; and a bookcase whose contents defy any title other than Martha's Stuff. Our new bookcase is called College. It will be the bookcase that sees the most action this year.

Already it is filling up with slick brochures that annoy me when I see the astronomical tuitions inside and wonder how much of my money will go toward marketing. We have every college-rating book on the market. My daughter is amassing all the necessary scores and keeping a running list of her achievements. Every time she does something remotely good, we say, "Oh, quick, add it to the list." There is a pageful of schools we will visit this fall, where my daughter will stay over in dorms to sample college life, and my husband and I will stay in cheap motels to sample life once we are financially ruined by having a child in college.

For monetary reasons, I attended a state university. I lived at home for my first years, and then with my husband in an apartment off campus. My sole purpose in college was to get good enough grades to be accepted into a clinical psychology doctoral program. I had no other college life. When I started having fun in graduate school, I realized what I had missed. I swore that I would do everything in my power to ensure that my children could go to college *wherever* they wanted.

Since the very beginning of our college explorations, however, it's been clear that I never really meant "wherever they wanted." I meant "wherever *I* wanted." I salivated at the facilities of the first two prestigious women's colleges we visited. I saw the young women in library carrels working late into a cold Sunday night and wished I were they. Throughout the tours, I exclaimed so much that my husband had to elbow me a couple of times. I directed my daughter's attention to the incredible labs, the spacious theaters, the excellent faculty. She agreed that all those things were impressive but found one major and insurmountable problem with both colleges. There were, as she so eloquently expressed it, "no guys."

"*Guys?*" I repeated, horrified. "Who cares about guys?"

"I do," she insisted.

She was making this declaration *after* we had flown to Massachusetts, rented a car, and booked hotel rooms.

"You couldn't have picked that up from the *catalog?*" I hissed, smiling at every admissions person who walked by.

"No," she replied. "I had to get a feel for what it would be like."

"Oh," I answered sarcastically, "and what does it *feel* like?"

"Well, I guess you could say that it pretty much sucks."

Then I quoted her the research on women's colleges and the fact that single-sex education appears to be good for young women.

"Mom," she argued, "I have always gone to school with guys. The presence of guys has never made me hold back, not show my smarts, not fight it out. I don't care what the research on women's colleges says. I want a place with guys."

I hammered away with the various reasons that she should reconsider. Every time she canceled an argument, I had a response.

Finally, my husband cut in, "Martha, stop it. This isn't about Keara. It's about *you. You* want to go there!"

He was right. I wanted my child to do this so that vicariously I could experience something I'd missed. That's the tricky part about having children. There's this need to have your children do, or undo, something that you never quite got right as a kid.

Because I never worked up to my academic potential until college, I've been vigilant about it in my daughter. I assumed that my coasting through grade school and high school was somehow attributable to my parents. They hadn't paid enough attention or done the right things. I smugly determined that with my own children, I would do it differently. But despite every damn thing I've done to block the repetition of that trend, my daughter has done exactly the same thing. I cannot bear one more discussion with a well-meaning young teacher who tells me that my daughter is a gifted but disorganized, inconsistent, and often academically indifferent child. I want to yell at them, *I've heard this so much it's like telling me that she's a five-foot-five-inch white female with red hair.*

My perceptions of my daughter are essentially distorted because they are filtered through the lens of *me.* Through that lens, she is the child who will repeat my goodness and undo my badness. She will be the things I never was—either because I wouldn't or because I couldn't. She will walk confidently down the paths I have cleared for her. She will deftly avoid my mistakes—the dangerous curves, the frightening spills, even the piles of dog shit I stepped in along the way. She will be smarter, more athletic, prettier, thinner, more adventurous, more ambitious, more successful. Her life will redeem mine.

There is just one problem with this plan. My daughter has absolutely no intention of redeeming anyone but herself. Depending on her mood, she laughs or yells at me when I try to impart my wisdom about college application forms. When I make suggestions about her applications, I add that *as a college professor,* I have experience she would do well to heed. I emphasize the fact that many people her age have gone *out of their way* to tell me that they found my advice extremely useful. But she receives this with less enthusiasm than when I offer my considerable talent as a child psychologist. She has let me know that she is going to do the applications *her* way and that my experience as a professor and psychologist is no more helpful in that process than if I were a dogcatcher or a stonemason.

For so long, I've thought that the beginning of her senior year would mark the point at which we had exactly one year left before "The Separation." I've always thought of separation as an *event*— the moment in time when we cry our good-byes, tearfully close car doors, and drive off leaving our only child behind in a strange and very expensive place. But now I know that our separation has already begun. I should have been more prepared. Because in some way, we have been moving toward it since her very first separation, when she was lifted out of my body to breathe, feel, and taste the world on her own. Echoes of my two-year-old girl who always wanted to "DOITBYMYSELF!" have returned, with even greater emphasis. When she was two, it was cute. Now it is painful.

I want my daughter to go, but I also want her to stay. She can't do both. Our feelings of closeness are so tangled up in our need to be separate. Sometimes in a crowded parking lot, she still smacks my hand away as it instinctively reaches out to guide her to safety. At other times, she surprises me when she spontaneously links arms with me in public and leans her head momentarily on my shoulder, making me feel like Queen of the World.

Our ambivalence about this parting is already playing itself out. The brush fires between us are increasing. My will and hers, which once blended so effortlessly, are now at odds. And it doesn't take much for us to ignite. She is condescending as she makes her haughty pronouncements about all aspects of my behavior, ideas, and appearance. She recently evaluated a suit I bought for a party by saying, "Well, Mom, everyone will know you're a writer." Thinking it was a compliment, I smiled, until she finished her commentary, "Because they'll know you are not involved in anything remotely resembling fashion."

Ten minutes after a barb like that, she is the little girl who can't fall asleep, who hugs me with a certain desperation and asks why everything can't just stay the same. She looks for my approval of her haircut, for reinforcement of her tentative pleasure with her newly conditioned body, for sharing her indignation as she reads her section of the newspaper aloud while I am trying to read mine in groggy silence.

In a question-and-answer session during a recent college visit, one nervous mother asked endless questions about how much supervision her son would receive in his dorm, what provisions the school made for emergencies, and whether there would be a safe place for her son to store his bicycle. There was a good bit of shifting in seats and rolling of eyes. Despite pressure from the parents who wanted to know the *really important* information, such as what percentage of graduates get into medical school and how many alumni are in Fortune 500 companies, the woman pursued her quest for reassurance. Her most urgent question was, "How will my son's laundry get done?" There were many superior smiles and sarcastic glances among the rest of us in that room. In my head I thought, *Lady, if you are asking a question like that, maybe you should consider the possibility that you and your son are not yet ready for the college experience.* On the way home, we laughed about the woman's pathetic anxiety and smugly congratulated ourselves for being above all that pathological worry.

But I am a hypocrite. Lately, I too have been hit with small waves of panic. What will she do about her asthma? Who will calm her down when she has procrastinated until she feels the walls closing in? Who will listen to her rambling stories? Who will understand that she needs the time and the space to be alone, to regroup? I wonder, Did I ever teach her to sew? I fear that her idea of mending and hemming will be driving to the dry cleaner's. I know I never taught her about laundry specifics such as bleach, fabric softeners, and washing machine cycles. All she knows is how to separate the light stuff from the dark stuff. Even if I wanted to, I couldn't teach her more, since that's all I know. I feel like I'm facing the final exam in Parenting 101 and I've realized that I missed too many classes. My daughter is a work-in-progress. I have trouble even sending the fifth or sixth draft of my writing out into the world. Keara is my one and only draft. How will I ever send *her* out?

I am on alert these days, ready to flow in and out of the many relationships that connect us. She is still my newborn child—the sweetest eight-pound gift of grace a person could receive. She is the baby who chafed at change and howled so loudly at bath time that the only way I could wash her was to lay her in the inflatable baby tub, bend over, curl one arm under her head and neck, stick my nipple in her protesting little mouth, and then soap her up with my other hand. Fortunately, the simultaneous feeding-and-washing routine was not required for too long. But part of my job as a mother has always been to ease her into new situations, to find ways in which the scary or unappealing may become tolerable, to bolster her sense that she can in fact do it, that it certainly won't kill her, and that she may end up even enjoying it.

She is still sometimes my three-year-old dynamo who demonstrated her ability to read by loudly pronouncing the obscenities scrawled on a storefront and innocently asking what they meant. In those early years, I fed her insatiable little head with information, encouraged play and the formation of friendships, and taught her how to tolerate life on the outside, away from Mom and Dad.

She is still sometimes my industrious elementary-school girl—the Brownie, the softball player, the clown, the Catholic, the student, the hungry reader, the enthusiastic friend. In those later years I began to move to the back of the bus, to encourage her independence and achievement, to transport, chaperone, accompany, organize, and quiz.

My adolescent girl has not erased her earlier selves. She has absorbed them. At seventeen, she is all of them. She is the young woman who adores field hockey, intellectual trivia, French films, vintage clothing, books, and feminism. She is a devout vegetarian, living in the midst of two hopeless carnivores. She is a less devout Catholic, questioning and searching in a church that encourages neither. She drives a car. She travels to places I've never seen.

Loving my daughter makes it hard to consider her leaving. Liking her makes it excruciating. In order for her to pack her bags, move into a dorm, and stay put, she and I are going to have to pull back a bit from each other. And one of the best ways to accomplish this is through the normal irritation, annoyance, and outright anger that come with the territory of separation. I have been working too hard to smooth over our growing differences, and that is unfair. Who wants to leave a place where everything is wonderful? Tension and friction are the fuels that power our ability to stand back from each other, to head off in different directions, to consider the fact that maybe what lies ahead out there in the distance is better than the sure thing you hold in your hands.

What I am supposed to do with my daughter now is not so different from what I did with the baby girl who wailed in distress at bath time seventeen years ago. Despite our mutual fears and protestations, I have to ease her into the water once again. Gently and slowly, so that she will hardly recognize the precise moment she shifts from land to water. And when she registers the fear, I will hold her close. She will remember once again how to love the water, and I will remember what a joy it is to see her swim.

❧ MODESTY

THE FACT THAT WOMEN who endured twelve to sixteen years of Catholic schools are not all virgins or prostitutes is a miracle.

The first time I consciously registered the word *sex*, I heard it from a nun. I was ten years old. It was my confirmation day. All fifth-grade girls were herded into the auditorium before the morning mass. We shivered in our lightweight polyester white gowns with red satin collars and ridiculous red beanies, ready to become "soldiers in the army of Christ." We had been instructed to wear white shoes and clear stockings. In addition, we were informed that for purposes of "modesty," which I thought meant not bragging about yourself and therefore didn't understand, we were required to wear long, full slips under our gowns. My economy-minded mother responded that it was ridiculous for prepubescent girls (whatever that meant) to be required to wear full slips. And, as the queen of improvisation, she made me try one of her half-slips with one of my regular undershirts. To say that I thought I would die is an understatement. While she was usually immune to protestations of what "every other girl" was doing, she must have registered the absolute terror on my face, because she relented. We bought a full slip, stockings, a garter belt, and flat white shoes.

The stockings and garter belt, which I had long coveted, turned out to be a huge pain in the ass, and I was relieved by the prospect of being able to return to plain socks the next day. I practiced walking in my new white shoes, consciously scuffing them on the sidewalk to prevent the occurrence of the inevitable fall whenever one hundred children walk on highly polished tile in brand-new shoes. At least one person in the class always took a sliding, flying fall in those processions. Most moments of embarrassment are felt far more personally than publicly. While they live on painfully in our own memories, most observers forget them almost immediately after they happen. But despite whatever the poor kid's parents said to comfort her or him—that it was no big deal and would be forgotten by the next day—my guess is that 98 percent of my class can still remember who took flight at our first communion.

Actually, we had two winners that year—Virginia Greeley and Marvin Miller.

Virginia took the spill, topped immediately by Marvin, who accepted his first host and then vomited in front of the entire congregation. He puked all over the highly polished tile floor and his bright white jacket, shirt, short pants, white kneesocks, white shoes, and even his little white bow tie. Other parents commiserated that it was probably the fasting. His parents claimed he had the flu. I figured he gagged on the wafer. If the priest put it way back on your tongue, it could stick to the roof of your mouth, which is why most kids come back from their first communion looking like they are rolling marbles in their mouths. The body of Christ can be difficult to swallow. Those kids are usually trying to dislodge a wafer, not having learned that you had to wait for a little saliva to soften it before you swallowed it. Otherwise, it was like trying to swallow a poker chip.

For the people still embarrassed and teased about their first-communion faux pas, confirmation offered the opportunity to be eclipsed by the next poor kid who would undoubtedly make his or her unique mark on the ceremony and would be taunted with it until eighth-grade graduation.

On the morning of our confirmation, the nuns lined us up by size, warning that they were going to conduct a full-slip inspection. The air in that room was electric with anxiety. Most of us were just at the point where we didn't want anyone to see us under our clothes, not even our mothers. Two nuns traveled down the line ferreting out the girls in half-slips. Offenders were yanked from the line and sent home in disgrace, causing them to miss the morning mass. They would be allowed to participate in the sacrament of confirmation that afternoon, provided they demonstrated proof of a full slip. I couldn't understand the concern. I didn't even know what they were so afraid that people would see. After the instant relief, a collective shame descended upon the rest of us, knowing that those girls were being punished for having something that we *all* had—only we had been more successful in covering it. The crime was not about the full slip. It was about what was under it.

We were instructed to sit down. Sister Carmelita delivered a lecture about what a holy day it was. I'll never forget her next sentence: "This is definitely not a day to be thinking about sex." *Sex,* I thought, *what's that?* It is hard to believe these days, when even three-year-old girls want to be "sexy," that we were so clueless about that word. But we were. Since second grade I had heard the euphemisms—immodest, impure, cheap, loose, dirty. But they had only the vaguest meaning.

In the paradoxical way that being told *not* to do something makes doing it so much more attractive, I thought about the sex thing all day. It connected with less conscious memories of the word overheard in whispers among the eighth-grade girls, or on the playgrounds with the older boys. It connected in some diffuse way to the general sense that becoming a full-grown woman was not an altogether good thing. The vigilance against betraying a woman's normal, healthy body was not stated outright to us yet. No one ever said, "Women are filth," although many of the scriptural references, such as making the name *woman* (as represented in Eve) synonymous with "the fall of man," came close. Saint Paul's blatant misogyny was recited from the pulpit without anyone trying to give it a context or qualify it in any way. The horrible things that those romantic women saints did to their developing bodies, in the name of Christ, would probably have appalled him. The sense of impending shame connected with the church's obsession with virginity, another word I still didn't understand but knew was related *only* to women and was paired with words like *immaculate, pure,* and *without sin.*

I knew it in the prohibition against "touching yourself." I knew it in the confused shame I felt after being harshly censured by a nun for linking pinkies with a favored friend. As we walked around the school yard, swinging our arms held together by our smallest fingers, she came up behind us and yelled, "What are you girls doing?"

"Nothing, Sister." Which was true.

"You will stop that immediately."

"Stop what, Sister?" I laughed anxiously, thinking that maybe she was kidding.

"Don't ever let me see you touching another girl in that way again."

What way?

But it connected most deeply for me in seeing how the church treated my mother. She steamed for weeks after a priest, from the pulpit, warned that women were bordering close to the brink of immodesty by wearing shorts. Not shorts *in church,* shorts in general. He wasn't talking about short, short cheek-huggers, either. He was talking about the kind of long, baggy Bermuda shorts that my mother had worn since childhood. For good measure, he also deemed sleeveless blouses and dresses immodest. My mother was usually reticent about criticizing the church in front of us. But as the priest spoke, I saw her hand—the one that didn't have a baby in it—stiffen around the pew in front to her. I could see her back straighten and her head tilt back, with her chin jutting out just a little in that wonderfully silent way of saying, *Yeah, and what are you gonna do about it?* She was quiet on the walk home. As we all retired to our separate rooms to change out of our church clothes, I could hear my mother behind her bedroom door. Despite the whispering, I could tell she was furious, and that my father was in total agreement. Hearing my parents break ranks with the church always gave me tremendous pleasure, and pride in knowing that I was on the right team. I heard my father say, "Pompous ass," which appeared to soothe my mother. She emerged several minutes later in a pair of plaid Bermuda shorts and a white sleeveless blouse.

But the worst was still to come. My mother was active in many aspects of the life of our parish, including teaching high-school Sunday school. Every week she let me grade the regular multiple-choice quizzes using a red pencil and the answer key from her textbook. It was much better than coercing my sisters and brothers into playing school. I loved marking older kids wrong. But in the middle of the year, my mother was "let go," which was a difficult thing for a Sunday school to do. It's not as if people were lined up waiting for those jobs. It was suggested to my mother that it would be better "for all concerned" if she withdrew from teaching for the rest of the year. I couldn't understand it. My mother was one of the smartest people I knew, capable of running a company, let alone a classroom. I knew kids who'd had her as a teacher and liked her. Why?

My mother was forced into an early retirement because she was pregnant—the Catholic way: five children in ten years. But I still didn't understand why that warranted early "retirement." When I asked my mother, she grimaced and answered, "Because I'm showing." My mother was pregnant so much, she was always "showing" as far as I was concerned. I didn't realize that those wise priests had determined that the vision of my mother standing in front of a high-school class would, in an "in-your-face" kind of way, be saying to her students, "Guess what I did to look like this?" No one even made a pretense of telling my mother that it was for *her*—take some time off, put your feet up. My mother carried children and grocery bags. She lugged baskets of laundry to the clothesline. She carried out the garbage, and she pushed the lawn mower. Nothing was said about what my mother might need. She wasn't "let go" for her. It wasn't for her students. It was for *them.* And even I knew it.

✿ TINKER BELL GETS HER PERIOD

AT ELEVEN, when I finally got up the nerve to question my mother about sex, I was instantly sorry. It was one of those moments so awful I can still remember exactly where I was sitting and exactly what my mother and I were wearing. She led me into her room and pulled out a paper and pencil from her bedside drawer. All of a sudden she was drawing fallopian tubes and talking about follicles and menstruation. I remembered the nun's admonition at my confirmation. Why would *anyone* be interested in this stuff? Ten diagrams, fifteen minutes, and considerable discomfort later, she asked me if I had any questions. I could tell she thought she was doing a really forthright job, but I couldn't handle any more information. I did, however, ask whether there was *any* way to avoid the entire situation. Since kindergarten we had been having this same discussion about death, with my mother as the voice of reason telling me that it was inevitable, and me always scheming for the "out" that might prove the exception. By the look on my mother's face, I knew that this was the same deal.

Several weeks later, my mother and I attended an animated Disney-like movie along the lines of "Tinker Bell gets her period." I don't remember too much of it because I was so incredibly embarrassed to be in a public place with my mother watching that film. I half-expected the cops to come in and break it up. I remember more footage of the follicles, ovaries, and fallopian tubes, with considerable detail on menstruation itself. There were several mentions of "very rare minor discomfort" and something about not having to stay in bed. Just when I thought it couldn't get worse, the leaders handed out boxes to all the girls. At first I thought it would be cool stuff, like party favors, to take the sting out of the evening. I made the mistake of ripping mine open right there. It was "feminine protection": a booklet, "sanitary napkins" (a frightening phrase), and a stupid little belt. And even though they served Hawaiian Punch and Pepperidge Farm cookies, which we never had at our house, I wanted to evaporate.

The next day at school, we could barely look one another in the eye. It was a silent recognition that, while we had all been initiated into the same society, admitting it in the light of day would just increase the shame. I wondered to myself if nuns menstruated. I wondered if my grandmothers menstruated. And worst of all, I wondered if men knew about it.

It took a while for us to talk to one another about it. My friends and I pooled woeful bits and scraps of information we had scavenged from various sources—older sisters, eavesdropping, "condemned" movies, magazines. This usually involved a competition about who had the most disgusting information. We huddled on the blacktop, and in response to each girl's revelation, we would choke and gag, pretend to be hit by a bullet or to vomit—all ending with a chorus of "That is sooo disgusting!" We still didn't exactly have sex and all this becoming-a-woman stuff down too well. The girls with the older sisters eventually introduced the issue of males into the whole framework—and we finally began to get the concept of "doing it." This won the all-time most-disgusting-revelation award, with the possible exception of Mrs. White getting a tampon stuck inside her and having to go to a doctor to have it taken out. I finally understood what had confused me for years—the neighborhood dogs who all of a sudden began howling and looking like they were glued together and Mr. Burgess cursing and spraying them with a garden hose until they separated. I'd always wondered what "heat" meant. And the puppies that followed later. *Oh my God,* I realized, *that's what our parents did.*

When it came to sex, I had the sense that we were thrown a bunch of puzzle pieces but were missing the most crucial pieces, as well as the instructions. One day, standing with our bikes following a ride to the neighborhood park, we pondered the fine points of where babies came from. Those of us with the largest families were accused of having parents who "did it" the most. But then we remembered that the nuns were always telling us that it is *God* who decides the frequency and timing of babies. We finally arrived at the point where we acknowledged, albeit reluctantly, that "doing it" had to take place at least once to produce children. I reasoned that you "did it" once on your wedding night, and that left you open for the rest of your life for children. This seemed to satisfy everyone, and it was unanimously added to our sexual-knowledge base.

At the end of sixth grade I began to understand what the big deal was. Paul Juliani, who had lived down the street from me for six years, all of a sudden looked interesting in a way that I couldn't shake. I began to feel stupid around him. By seventh grade, our relationship had taken on a combative flavor—as a way of interacting, safely. We made faces at each other in class and began to exchange notes written the night before. In our notes, we combined random words pulled from the dictionary to form a paragraph. Then the other one had to wait to get home to decode it. The message was always total nonsense, but the pleasure in it was enormous. It was a wonderful way to communicate intensely without actually saying a blessed thing. I remember only one sentence from our many exchanges: "Our cahoots are formidable." Our blossoming association concerned our teacher enough that she called my mother with the news that Paul walked me home. My mother loved telling the nun that since our family lived farthest away, it was actually *I* who walked Paul home. Warnings forbidding "boy-girl parties" were sent home to parents. Fortunately, a number of parents didn't agree with this prohibition and allowed them anyway.

To combat the mutiny, our teachers decided it was time for the combination human-sexuality and burn-in-hell lecture. The nuns didn't do this one. For this, the heavy cavalry was called in—pretty much the only time priests visited the school. Father Redmond, rather bumbling anyway, must have been the lowest in the priests' hierarchy, because he got the job. After math, the boys and girls were separated (which was always a sign that something juicy was about to happen). First, he dealt with the boys while Sister Ambrose, one of two nuns who made the entire experience of grade school worthwhile, read "The Tell-Tale Heart" by Edgar Allan Poe to the girls.

Eventually, a defeated-looking Father Redmond shuffled into our classroom as though he were doing the greatest penance of his life. And he was right to be afraid. I have yet to see a priest walk into a roomful of adolescent girls and not be sweetly but summarily crucified by them if they wanted to. And this guy was fish bait. He stood sweating in front of us, organizing his little index cards and looking like he'd prefer speaking to hundreds of people from the distance of the high altar rather than to fifty seventh-grade girls up close in a sweaty classroom. He gave a long rambling talk filled with phrases like *conjugal love* and *the marital act.* I don't know what he thought we were doing, but he seemed very concerned. We were almost wetting our pants, knowing that we had a live one on the line. He wrote things on the board. Then he'd turn and lean against it, trying to look cool—throwing a piece of chalk up in the air but missing it on its return trip, which left him scrambling around on the floor trying to find it. When he turned around, we could see "marital act" written in chalk backward on his black priest suit. My neck and chest hurt from stifling so much laughter.

He should have known to leave it right there. But he made the fatal error of asking us to write down our questions—"any questions at all, girls" (big mistake)—on index cards . . . anonymously (bigger mistake). He collected them solemnly, and we watched him squirm as he looked at the first card, blanched, and put it on the bottom of the pile. He repeated this sequence a number of times and then decided on the best of the worst to answer.

Was French-kissing a mortal sin? Yes.

How much of a tongue has to be in a mouth to qualify as a true French kiss? Approximately one-fourth of an inch.

What is the difference between light and heavy petting? Light petting involves the upper regions. Heavy petting involves the lower regions.

Can a boy tell if you are having your period by kissing you? No.

Does the pope have a "thing"? Yes, but he doesn't use it.

Does God have a "thing"? If not, how did Mary get pregnant? No, God does not have a "thing." Mary's pregnancy requires an act of faith.

Mary Ann Williams snickered in the back row, "Yeah, especially for Joseph."

This totally flustered him. "Well, girls, I think that's enough for today. We will cover the rest of these topics at another time," which we knew meant never, if he could help it. He concluded with two helpful hints for warding off impure thoughts and deeds: "Imagine that our Holy Father is standing right there watching you at all times" and "Imagine you are in a plane that is about to crash—because that is exactly what's happening to your soul."

❧ PURE

IN THE MIDDLE of seventh grade, boys and girls who had stayed as far away from each other as possible began, slowly, to converge. A well-defined circle of girls integrated a well-defined circle of boys. During the school day, we often acted as if nothing had changed, which was fairly easy to accomplish given the segregation of the sexes in any free-form activity. After school, we rode our bikes to our meeting place—a room in Catherine Farnsley's garage. We spent hundreds of hours there, talking, experimenting with cigarettes and alcohol, and falling in love with each other. I was taken by the storytelling of boys—its energy, blunt humor, and bullshit. Their stories differed from the stories of girls, where the emphasis was on capturing feelings and moments, figuring people out, analyzing situations, and honing the fine-tuned art of bitchiness—with ourselves, and most of all, with people outside of "us."

I fell in love with Benjamin Quinn in that garage. He was tall, smart (but not too smart), and athletic, which I already knew to be an asset in a male. But most of all, I fell in love with him because he fell in love with me. I practiced writing "Mrs. Benjamin Quinn" in the margins of my notebook, despite the fact that I had insisted for years to my mother that I would never give up my own name. I fantasized about kissing him, but nothing much ever happened. My other friends were equally frustrated. The myth of the predatory male, from whom we should carefully guard our virtue, was not holding up. The only physical contact we had with these boys was the same contact they had with one another—arm and thumb wrestling, punches on the shoulder, games of "Uncle." Fun, but what we'd been reading about in *Teen* and *Seventeen* was considerably more romantic.

Because we all shared the understanding that it was the boy who made "the first move" and that the worst way a girl could be perceived was as "forward" (precursor to "slut"), we realized that we had to nudge the situation along indirectly.

We devised a form of spin-the-bottle in which, eventually, everyone would have to kiss everyone else, thereby breaking the ice and allowing us to pair off. My first kiss was a public one. Benjamin gallantly removed a wad of Bazooka bubble gum from his mouth, and we engaged in your basic teeth-banging, lip-bruising, sorry excuse of a kiss. But as he kissed me, Ben raised his hand and two of his fingers lightly grazed my face. At that moment, all the dormant energy that had been bubbling below the sexual surface of our lives was activated. A switch was thrown. The houselights dimmed. And the show began.

By the summer after seventh grade, we were wild. We stole cigarettes from our mothers' purses and pooled liquor stolen from our houses, learning quickly how to dilute what was left so our parents wouldn't notice. Hanging out together for months gave us a familiarity with one another and permission to continue to push the boundaries together.

One boring, slow summer day, we hid from the sun and all people whom we deemed beneath us (which was everybody) in Catherine's garage. In the restlessness and the heat, we began to dare each other. The boys dared Kevin Connor to eat a live insect. He did. The girls dared Catherine to steal money from her mother's purse. She returned with a five-dollar bill but said she'd have to return it before her mother noticed. She was roundly booed and got only partial credit.

Next, they dared me to take my shirt off in front of Benjamin. Being dared is a dangerous thing for me. If it had been a suggestion, I would have dismissed it, but a dare was a different matter. A dare says: Let's see if you have it in you; put your money where your mouth is. While I was up for the adventure, I insisted on rules. Rule one: They all had to agree to leave us alone in the garage. Rule two: Look, but don't touch. Poor Benjamin, who hadn't been dared to do anything but watch, looked frightened. I felt a tremendous sense of power as I stood there facing him. He was wide-eyed and unblinking as I undid the three buttons of my madras shirt, slipped it over my shoulders, and reached over my head to pull it off.

The way he looked at me became its own dare. I wanted to take it further. I reached behind me and fumbled with the clasp of my 32A bra. Ben looked like he was losing oxygen. The bra released against my back, but I held it in place with my hands. Then, slowly, I let my arms fall to my sides and the bra fell to the floor.

Chasing Grace

And Benjamin stared like a blind man who's just been hit by lightning and regained his long-lost sight. I looked him in the eye and felt more powerful, more beautiful, and more desirable than I had ever felt before—and would ever feel again. He stared at me as I had seen people stare at Michelangelo's *Pieta* when it was exhibited at the New York World's Fair. He never tried to touch me. We both knew that this was much more significant than touching. We could hear our friends tapping at the blackened windows and getting a kick out of their vicarious walk in the ways of the wicked. Catherine's mother yelled from the house, "What's going on out there?" But I didn't feel guilty or hurried. It would not be long before I began the years of relentless sexual bargaining with boys—over the shirt, under the shirt but over the bra, under the bra, and so on. From there we would move around the bases, trying to keep the pleasure-to-sin ratio within manageable limits. But this one time was different.

I knew, from everything I had been taught, that I should definitely bring this to confession. But I didn't want to. Not because I was afraid. Because I wanted to cherish it, not confess it. That one time, it was pure. Before I was too brainwashed, before I learned to worry about my reputation, before all the ways I would learn how to hate my body, there was that moment. It was the Happy New Year before the Day of Atonement. It was "This is who I am, who I am becoming. It is a perfect offering and I am choosing you to receive it. You will be my first, one of many firsts. And in some way, I will always be yours."

❧ CHARM

MY PARENTS realized that, for me, attending to boys and attending to academics were close to mutually exclusive activities. They enrolled me in an all-girls Catholic high school. Very early on, it became apparent that high-school nuns were different from grade-school nuns. In grade school, the smart ones who were good teachers and decent human beings were in the minority. In high school, they were the majority. The high-school nuns were better educated and better schooled in the techniques of classroom control without the use of physical violence or public humiliation.

I attended high school in the late sixties, a time of tremendous change—in the country and in the church. While the changes of Vatican II were often difficult for the older nuns, the younger ones seemed energized by it. In general, high school emphasized *how* to think over *what* to think. This was much truer in political, social, and even theological realms, however, than it was in the last frontier—sexuality.

Freshman English was taught by Sister Augustine, a large, regal woman in her sixties, clearly from an aristocratic background and rumored to have been a fashion model in her youth. She pronounced "girls" as "guuulls," which we found rather exotic and imitated constantly in the locker room. One day a week, part of each class was devoted to a subject that was broadly defined as "charm." Sister Augustine told us that charm could compensate for the lack of anything, from good looks to brains. "In the end," she pronounced with authority, "a man will choose the charming woman over the beautiful woman, the intelligent woman, the wealthy woman, the loose woman."

Charm involved developing a large vocabulary with which one could engage anyone in stimulating conversation. Charm involved carefully ar—ti—cu—lat—ing those words by squeezing the last drop out of every syllable. She taught us how to breathe from our diaphragms as we spoke, and led us in vocal exercises such as "zoooo, zeeee, zaaaa, zoooo, zuuuu." She insisted that they be pronounced with great exaggeration, making us sound and look more like trained chimps than charming young women.

Charm required knowing how to point. Wrist rotated, palm up, index finger sweeping out from one's midsection to one's right. It involved knowing that a pair of clean white cotton gloves compensated for any number of wardrobe deficiencies. Charming girls never chewed gum, teased their hair, wore earrings that hung below their ears, or laughed without covering their mouths.

Charm involved keeping men interested, but at a safe distance. Sister Augustine knew instinctively that we would need help in this area and never relied on words alone to make her point. Many hours were spent learning and practicing charming behaviors. With partners playing the roles of boys, we practiced staring at them haughtily until they opened the car doors or pulled out chairs for us. We practiced sitting down, carefully smoothing our skirts before depositing our butts on the chair. We practiced standing up. The main goal in the entire endeavor was to keep your legs glued together at absolutely all times.

The most challenging of situations involved getting out of a car as a boy was holding the door open for you. She warned us solemnly that while our "young men" no doubt would be innocently performing their duties as gentlemen, they also had a tremendous opportunity to look up our dresses. They could be prohibited from this if we slammed our legs together as they slammed their car doors, swung our entire bodies to an immediate, swift right, and then stood up as quickly as possible once they opened the door for us. We practiced this many times, but most of us still never got it right.

Sister Augustine loved to make impromptu pronouncements, usually with some kind of moral fable in which a well-meaning but careless girl neglected the basics of stellar young womanhood and ruined her life forever. She had several issues that she could not stress enough. In the same breath in which she told us that the apocryphal prohibition against black patent-leather shoes (because they reflect up) was "rubbish," she warned us to be mindful that the color white made boys think of bedsheets. We could have pointed out to her that white was the color we wore at our baptisms, first communions, and confirmations, and what we would hopefully wear at our weddings. But it was easier sometimes just to say, "Yes, Sister," and write it all down.

Sister Augustine told us never, never to sit on a boy's lap. By high school, we were all experts in the legal technicalities of Catholic "nevers." Ten hands shot up with various exceptions. She had an easy answer for everything. Her biggest challenge came from Susanna Morgan, who asked, "Sister, what if you're at a party way, way out . . . miles away from your house . . . and the friends you came with . . . left you . . . and you tried to call . . . your parents . . . but there was no answer . . . and did I say already that the house was surrounded by woods . . . and the only car left . . . has boys in it . . . and they offer you a ride . . . but the car is already full . . . and the only way to get home . . . is to sit . . . on one of their . . . laps?" We could tell that this was a tough one by the considerable thought Sister devoted to it. But she brightened after several moments of reflection and pronounced, "Choose the least attractive young man and put a phone book between the two of you."

Caught between disbelief and hilarity, neither of which was charming, or allowed, we deferred all questions about the obvious problem of phone book availability and its consequences. The bell rang. We swung ourselves out of our desks with our legs wide open and bolted for the door as Sister Augustine sang out, "Guuulls . . . remember . . . use those diaphragms!"

❧ RELEVANCE

AT THE OTHER END of the freshman-year continuum was religion with Sister Miriam.

She was a well-meaning, nervous little woman with skin so pale you could see every vein in her hand. My best guess is that during the summer break Sister Miriam had attended some kind of workshop on teaching religion to adolescents. There was a major focus in the mid-sixties on making Catholicism "relevant" to its indigenous subcultures—adolescents being one of them. This resulted in the creation of "rap groups" for teenagers. The intention was admirable, but its translation into action was problematic. In describing the structure of the course, Sister Miriam acted as if she were giving out the winning number of the next day's lottery when she told us that, on Fridays, we would "rap."

No one had the heart to tell the poor woman that middle-class white girls didn't "rap." We knew we weren't cool enough to rap. We talked, we bitched, we moaned. But we definitely didn't rap. She asked us what would make the class "meaningful" to us. Any teacher who asks her class that question has to know that she has just entered the give-them-an-inch-and-they'll-take-a-mile zone.

Nancy Meaney proposed food as something meaningful. It obviously wasn't even close to what Sister Miriam had in mind, but she wanted to reinforce any participation and agreed that we could have food. "Anything else?" she asked hopefully. "Music would be good," offered Elizabeth Byrne. Sister Miriam winced and repeated, "Music?" Elizabeth then told the class how the boys' high school a few miles away had "Record Day," when kids brought in records and played them for the class. Then they broke up into small groups to discuss the "theological, moral, and social" implications of the song. Elizabeth Byrne could bullshit with the best of them. When Sister Miriam heard that people were doing it at another Catholic high school, she perked right up and agreed to it immediately.

For the first few weeks, we played it cool—Joni Mitchell, "Both Sides Now"; Simon and Garfunkel, "The Sounds of Silence"; the Byrds, "To everything . . . turn, turn, turn, there is a season." Straight out of Ecclesiastes. We manufactured weighty discussions as Sister Miriam floated around the room listening to each group "rap." As soon as she was gone, we'd get back to the real subject, which usually focused on what we were going to do that weekend.

Martha Manning

Record Day deteriorated over time, forcing the participants to really stretch the relevance of the chosen songs. Just as it seemed that every piece of literature we read in high school had a "Christ figure," we were always able to find some shred of Catholicism in just about any piece of music. But after six weeks or so, we grew weary of the tortured introspection of folksingers.

When it was my turn, I went right to the top and brought in the Queen of Soul herself. I figured you couldn't get any closer to God than that. The instant that Aretha got going into high gear with "Ain't gonna do you wrong . . . ," Sister Miriam almost leapt out of her seat. The throbbing sexual intensity of that song made it impossible even for Sister Miriam to sit still. She inched closer to the record player, just in case things got out of control. You could see her pulse racing in her tiny blue veins, and her face began to turn "a whiter shade of pale." Someone started to sing backup, "Whip it to me . . . ," and it was all over. Thirty white girls got religion. We sang out "Sock it to me, sock it to me, sock it to me," moving in ways the nuns never saw when we stood erect in the auditorium and sang anthems like "Sacred Heart we sing to thee, pledging our fidelity" (we always substituted "virginity"), raising our right arms in a stiff salute, like Hitler Youth, as we sang, "Hail from your daughter's Sacred Heart." It's just hard to get worked up over songs like that.

Sister Miriam and I did not share the same assessment of what constituted "soul" music. Despite the fact that "Respect" actually promoted the best discussion we'd had so far—about self-respect, about boys getting in the way, about demanding what you think is right—Sister Miriam determined Aretha to be "inappropriate." She turned hopefully to Janet Reedy, the other girl assigned to be that week's Record Day contributor. Unfortunately, Janet's selection was "Love Child" by Diana Ross—in theory an excellent choice: "No, I won't have sex with you because I was born a bastard and I won't do that to anyone else." But we were already over the top. Sister Miriam had maxed out on relevance. We could have had the pope singing "Ave Maria" and it wouldn't have helped. Record Day was canceled. For the rest of the term, we watched filmstrips of the Holy Land every Friday—without food. Relevance was dead.

❧ HOT DOGS

FOR TEN YEARS, we had been educated, indoctrinated, frightened, threatened, and confused in the realm of human sexuality. It was hard not to come out of that time with a sense that the church had nothing resembling a positive attitude about sex. Sex was an unfortunate means to a necessary end—procreation. And that was it.

But in tenth grade, our teachers took a 180-degree turn on the whole issue of sex. All of a sudden, sex was beautiful. Sister Loretta taught the "Family Life" (euphemism for "sex") segment of our religion class. On the entire faculty they could not have chosen a teacher with less credibility in the area of sex. Sister Loretta was a gentle soul, one of those nuns who was so good and so holy that her feet never seemed to touch the ground. It was fairly obvious that at fifteen we had more sexual experience—in thought, word, and deed—than sweet Sister Loretta, who was probably in her early thirties.

Now, *intimacy* was the code word for sex. Sister Loretta waxed poetic about the gifts of God in a relationship between a husband and wife. She would sail across the room, smiling so beatifically that no one in good conscience could nail her.

"Girls, sex is beautiful," she sang, waving her graceful hands through the air as if she were talking about classical music, modern sculpture, or something equally boring. For us, sex wasn't beautiful. It was exciting, provocative, and daring. To think of it as beautiful somehow took all the fun out of it. However, we looked forward to several months of classes about human sexuality in which we would all earn A's, because we knew from experience that they had no intention of teaching us anything.

I am not by nature a paranoid person. But I have come to believe that what followed in those months was some of the most brilliant and devious strategizing in the history of Catholic education. Our teachers were just smart enough to know that their words and warnings meant nothing to us. And so they found other methods of shaping our attitudes and behaviors.

For the first month, we were overwhelmed and, frankly, pleased with the amount of basic, honest information about human development and reproduction. Not that it was all that much. My daughter was better educated by third grade than I was in tenth. The information became diffuse when it came to the part we were always waiting for—"doing it." Sister Loretta showed movies in which loving couples began hugging and kissing, and we'd get all excited that this time we were actually going to get to the good part. But we never did. The best film showed a young man and woman (the first non-nerds depicted in any of these films) walking arm and arm through a wheat field. In the next frame, they had three kids. You never even saw a bare arm. If you didn't already have something on the ball, you'd have been left wondering about cross-pollination or God dropping babies into wheat fields.

Just when the curriculum planners had us agreeing that yes, sex was in fact beautiful, they dropped the bomb. The last week was "speakers' week." It sounded innocent enough. Different women would come in to speak to us on topics related to the Family Life unit. Rather than meeting in our usual classroom, we were led to the music room by Sister Loretta. One look at the room told you that music was not a high priority at our school. It was dark, small, and poorly ventilated. We packed into the room and ended up shoulder to shoulder with the girls on either side of us.

The first speaker was Mrs. Claire Maloney from the Gwendolyn Farrington Home for Unwed Mothers. She gave a rather alarming talk about how teenage pregnancy totally ruins your life, makes you "used goods" to every subsequent male in your life, and isolates you from your baby, God, and society in general. She made "the home" sound less like a haven than an eighteenth-century orphanage. Because we were all still "technical virgins," it was initially fairly easy to distance ourselves from "those girls." But then Mrs. Maloney delivered the zinger, "And you girls out there who think you are safe just because there has been no *penetration*, think again. The Gwendolyn Farrington Home is *full* of girls who got pregnant without PENETRATION." I could feel people freeze all around me. *How is that possible?* we wondered. *Is she telling the truth? Oh my God, could I be pregnant?*

Mrs. Maloney concluded her speech, obviously satisfied that she had scared the shit out of us. Sister Loretta smiled innocently and sang out, "Girls, shouldn't we thank Mrs. Maloney?" It was a rhetorical question because she began clapping her hands in appreciation and looked at us with the expectation that we would do the same. Yeah, Mrs. Claire Maloney, thanks a lot. Because religion was the class before lunch, we had a chance to commiserate over the cafeteria's excuse for meat loaf. There were two lines of thinking: Mrs. Maloney was a bitch and she was lying, or Mrs. Maloney was a bitch and some of us were in deep shit. Everyone agreed she was a bitch, and after much discussion, we concluded, for our own peace of mind, that she was also a liar.

The next day, despite our loud complaints, we were ushered back into the music room. The morning's speaker was Mrs. Theresa Gallagher—a "homemaker and mother of ten," as Sister Loretta introduced her. Mrs. Gallagher had been invited to talk to us about birth control, which seemed a bit like inviting Attila the Hun to discuss good sportsmanship. Mrs. Gallagher's wisdom must have been gained in retrospect, since it was obvious that she hadn't applied it to her own childbearing years. But two minutes after she began talking, it was clear that Mrs. Gallagher was not going to teach us about using birth control. She was going to teach us about *not* using birth control. She was going to teach us about "accepting children lovingly from God," which meant countless children, with whatever timing, regardless of the context. To us it meant, "Kiss your twenties, your thirties, and even your forties good-bye." As an alternative she offered "natural family planning," which involved abstinence during high-risk days. Natural family planning sounded a lot like the rhythm method, which was probably responsible for the presence of at least half the girls in the room.

Mrs. Gallagher droned on and on about the added dimension that abstinence contributed to a marriage. The room was hot, and Nancy Farris kept leaning over and whispering under her breath, "Bullshit, bullshit . . . bullshit." She handed me her wallet opened to a picture she wanted me to see. It was a Polaroid of a headless guy on a motorcycle . . . with . . . his . . . thing . . . oh my God . . . his *really huge* thing . . . hard on the seat. I tried to cover my laughter with coughing until finally I really was coughing. Mrs. Gallagher invited me to leave the room for water. I threw the wallet back at Nancy and saw her handing it to Terry Moore on the other side of her.

Out in the hall at the water fountain I laughed all by myself for several minutes. Then I leaned against the wall for a while, enjoying the fresher, cooler air, until I recovered a modicum of self-control. By then I expected that the Polaroid would have made full rounds and that everyone would be in hysterics.

But when I walked back into the room, the girls looked horrified and ashen. The music room was hauntingly quiet. As I walked to my seat, I looked quizzically at a few of my friends. In response, they grimaced and pointed to the front of the room. It wasn't until I had settled into my seat that I understood why. It seemed that Mrs. Gallagher had brought along a visual aid. In a large jar, probably in formaldehyde, floated a four-month-old fetus. A fetus that, as Mrs. Gallagher described it, was called away early by God;

a fetus that she had expelled into her toilet. She then described how she immediately reached into the toilet and baptized the fetus.

I thought she was absolutely out of her mind, which was understandable, given the number of children she had. But Sister Loretta beamed, as if Mrs. Gallagher was showing us nothing more disturbing than a map of the United States.

Once again, we were forced to applaud a woman who made us sick. At lunch, we were not as jovial about dismissing Mrs. Gallagher as we had Mrs. Maloney the day before. We all thought she was a bitch. And Kathleen Curtain spoke for everyone when she folded her hands, looked up to heaven, and said, "Thank you, God, that she is not my mother." But no one was in the mood for levity. We had just seen our first dead baby. A real woman's real dead baby. And we were supposed to just eat our chicken-salad sandwiches, gather up our books, and dash to geometry as if nothing had happened. We all shuddered when Sarah Connally asked only half-jokingly, "Who do you think they'll drag in tomorrow?" It was hard to imagine how they could top Mrs. Gallagher.

But with the presentation of Nurse Richards, they proved it was possible. Mrs. Richards was the jewel in the crown. She was the final speaker on the final day of Family Life. Nurse Richards (she was introduced to us as if "Nurse" were her first name) was a stocky, I-don't-take-shit-from-anybody ex–Army nurse. She embodied the essence of the phrase *old battle-ax*. Nurse Richards stood erect before us, in uniform, ready to perform her mission— which, it turned out, was to teach us about childbirth. She told us she had never had children of her own but assured us that she had delivered "hundreds of 'em—all shapes, colors, and sizes."

Nurse Richards, another believer in visual aids, rolled out a movie projector. Sister Loretta fumbled with the screen. The already-dark room got darker. Our giggling and restlessness reflected a collective curiosity and anxiety about what was coming. The anxiety was appropriate. We were just about to be fed to the wolves. The first thing on the screen was one of those 1940s titles, with background music like in the weekly newsreels shown in movie theaters during the Second World War. "U.S. troops struck a major blow against the Germans. . . . On the sports front. . . ." Only this one was called *Emergency Childbirth: Delivering a Baby in a Disaster.*

It was unbelievable. The premise of the movie was that there was some kind of natural or nuclear disaster in which no one had access to anything but a bomb shelter, which, in this movie, looked more like a work shed. In between shots of a screaming pregnant woman were scenes in which the instruments needed for assisting a childbirth were articulated. Of course, since they were in a bomb shelter–work shed, they didn't have any of those things. Therefore, substitute labor and delivery instruments were recommended. A pair of hands was shown laying everything out on the table: garden shears, twine, hose, and newspaper. In the background the woman continued to heave and scream.

Seeing childbirth for the first time, even under the best conditions, as in prenatal classes, is often difficult for adults. Films with loving couples in beautifully appointed birthing rooms, surrounded by a loving obstetrical team and gorgeous background music, can still make the uninitiated pass out.

Emergency Childbirth was exactly the opposite. It represented birth under the worst possible conditions—a woman screaming in pain, attended by a faceless set of hands, in a bomb shelter, on a picnic bench covered with old newspapers, with a voice-over that sounded like it was announcing the daily farm report.

Suddenly, the camera zoomed in on the baby's head crowning between the screaming woman's legs. For ten years no one had been explicit with us about *anything* to do with sex, and then there, in *Emergency Childbirth,* they decided to get graphic. Several girls closed their eyes. Some of us covered our mouths as we groaned in time with the woman. We all knew there was pain in labor. We didn't know, however, about the screaming, pushing, tearing, gushing water, and blood.

That was all corrected in the next three minutes of footage when the baby, after one final horror-movie scream from the woman, slithered out into the waiting "hands." The lack of circulated air was oppressive. The delivery of the placenta coincided with Joanne Talbott's loss of consciousness. Mary Ellen Hanlon looked like she was going to puke and fled the room. The movie continued, with tips on how to tie off the cord and stitch up the mother. We didn't watch the rest. We endured it. Nurse Richards flicked on the lights, and the projector hummed for a while before totally stopping. I had never seen my classmates so shaken. Nurse Richards asked if there were any questions, knowing that there wouldn't be. We all sat there, reeling with the knowledge that "fooling around" could lead to this. Not just pregnancy, but emergency childbirth. No teacher had to say a word. It was supremely simple. They just had to let it sink in.

We shuffled into the cafeteria, defeated and upset, everyone making promises that whatever "son of a bitch" she was dating at the moment was never going to lay a hand on her again . . . ever. After that, we just sat there, silently absorbing the trauma of the previous fifty minutes.

For lunch that day, the cafeteria served hot dogs. No one touched them.

❧ MATCHING APPLIANCES

I LOVE watching couples. I always have. The only thing that has changed over the years is which ones I find interesting. I usually target couples whose relationship is "ahead" of mine. It's like watching previews in movies; I find it comforting to know what's in store. After being married for several years, I sighed wistfully as I watched new parents with their sweet babies. When I was the parent of a young child, I looked at parents of older children, using them as proof to myself that childhood is a treatable condition that abates with time. As a parent of an adolescent, now I'm looking at couples whose children have left for college or work, wondering why some of them look supremely relieved and free and others look lost, like they've been cut loose from a mooring.

When I was dating my husband-to-be in high school, I was fascinated with newlyweds. I adored weddings—even when I didn't know the people. The love expressed so openly, the hope, the long dresses and flowers evoked the fairy tales I had loved so much as a child. Through her association with "the prince," a girl is rescued, married, elevated, and eternally happy. Who wouldn't want that?

When I was sixteen, I saw marriage as the pinnacle in a woman's life, with motherhood a close second. In my fantasies, I never projected myself beyond the wedding. I had a vague sense that I would attend college, but only so that I could be a good mother to my children or have "something to fall back on" if my husband left me (as in "died"). I never even considered the possibility of divorce. Thoughts of an actual career did not cross my mind.

Ironically, it wasn't until I became engaged on my twentieth birthday that I started thinking about the rest of my life. The actual proposal of marriage—an event I had played out thousands of times in my head, each time more romantic, more spectacular—lasted eight and a half minutes, at most. There were no beautiful dress and tuxedo by candlelight in a wickedly expensive restaurant, with champagne and long-stemmed pale-peach roses, no Brian kneeling down professing his devotion, no dining room breaking into applause as I accepted, and no me radiant with joy for every single moment of the rest of my life.

In reality, we were in our wet, sandy bathing suits dripping on the hall carpet in my grandmother's beach house in the middle of the morning. There were no flowers, champagne, or applause. Just a simple opal ring I had admired months before and an unwavering and straightforward declaration of love.

Unlike the absolute perfection of the fantasy, my reaction to the reality of my engagement was ambivalent. I was thrilled. But I was also terrified. This was the rest of my life we were talking about. *My life.* MY LIFE. All of a sudden, I realized how little I'd thought about it that way. I'd jumped right over it to thoughts about *our life.* I had never actually calculated the total time spent in engagement fantasies, but I knew it was a hell of a lot more than the eight and a half minutes I had just experienced.

If this was the deal with engagement, was it also true for marriage? When we drove off in our "Just Married" car, lewdly decorated by our drunken friends, would it really be the beginning of our lives, or the end? I looked at my married friends in their cute little houses where everything was brand-new and the avocado refrigerator matched the stove and the blender. There were little soaps in the bathroom and pastel handtowels I was afraid to use. My friends were starting recipe boxes with cards that said "From the kitchen of . . ." They were sewing their own curtains, deciding on new linoleum, and calling their husbands "Honey." What looked so good before my engagement suddenly had more potential for claustrophobia than solitary confinement. As I sat across from a happy couple at dinner, I felt like we were all *playing* house more than we were *living* it. I had to stifle the urge to interrupt full-bodied conversations about lawn furniture or carpeting and scream: *Is this it? Is this what we do for the rest of our lives?*

I had the good sense to wait until we were back in the car before I actually started yelling. "If this is it," I declared, "then I don't want it."

"What is IT?" asked my perplexed fiancé.

"You know, all this marriage crap. How you get married and immediately turn boring. I can't handle the recipe cards, Brian. I just can't. And I don't see how a wedding ring will help."

Brian reassured me that he didn't see recipe cards in my future. But when I asked him what he did see, he couldn't answer. And worse, when he turned the question back to me, neither could I. I'd never thought about myself past about age twenty-five. By that time, I figured, I'd have my two beautiful children, a nice house, a successful husband. I would be set for life. But "set for life" was beginning to feel less like being surrounded by security and more like being surrounded by a straitjacket. Each time I tried to project myself further into my future, my image became diffuse. My features lost definition. I couldn't hear my own voice.

But somewhere between the day of my engagement and the day of my wedding, the picture became clearer. I wanted to go to graduate school before I had children. I had expectations about how we would both contribute to the support and running of our household. I intended to keep my name. I announced each of these declarations (and a whole list of others) to Brian as if they were articles of war ("Under the Equal Household Act of 1972"), challenging him to disappoint me. With each pronouncement, I drew a line in the dirt and dared him to step over it. But he refused to play that game.

Being able to struggle and state what I wanted helped me to see that it isn't marriage that limits people so much as their expectations about it. I finally relaxed when I realized that Brian and I could make the rest of it up as we went along. It took the promise of a lack of closure to bring me to closure.

The night before our wedding, with at least fifty family members getting a jump on the celebrating downstairs, Brian slumped back in my beloved lumpy reading chair and I sat cross-legged on my bed. The only thing left was to write our vows. A combination of fatigue and nerves contributed to several verses that would have prematurely terminated the ceremony. When we finally calmed down and really tried to write them, we realized why most people use the ones in the book.

It's hard to make promises to a person. Promises that will last. Promises that mean something to both people. Promises that you can bring to mind for direction in confusing or rotten times.

We struggled for several hours and yielded a total of only thirty-eight words. But they were words we could say with a straight face, and goals we believed were possible. The folk songs we chose twenty-two years ago now sound sappy or whiny. I understand now why Brian's father was so upset about his long hair. And I don't know what drugs I was taking when I decided on my bridesmaids' hats.

But the vows worked then and they still work now. They meant something different to me at twenty-one than they do at forty-three. When I said those words at twenty-one, resisting recipe cards, avocado appliances, and a boring life were the challenges I anticipated. When I first said those words, I never envisioned that they would have to stretch so far—over times of tremendous pain and suffering, over the wonderful and awful stages of parenthood, over advances we never expected and losses we'd always feared. I didn't know that they were meant as much for the "I hate you and anyone who looks like you" times as for the "I love you completely, passionately, and only" times. All I knew was that I meant them then and I wanted to mean them for the rest of my life. And the best thing is that I still do.

"I take you as my husband. I promise to love you always, to encourage you to realize all that you wish to become, and to share with you in the myriad of experiences that life together will offer."

It's been twenty-two years.

Still too soon to tell.

But so far, so good.

✻ GROCERY STORE

SATURDAY, in the early evening, is a terrible time to shop. The hard-core household shopping has already been done during the week or on weekend mornings by the responsible people.

Saturday evening is when people shop for fun. Often, it's not for the staples of life that get a family through the week. It's for the makings of a wonderfully creative and romantic meal. Shopping on Saturday evenings is foreplay.

I shop on Saturday evenings, but not because it's sexy. I shop then because I should have been one of the responsible people but I procrastinated. And now we don't even have to take a quick sniff of the carton to tell that the milk's sour. We just have to walk in the general direction of the kitchen. We're out of plastic garbage bags, and the floor is littered with many small paper bags, leaning against one another for support and overflowing with awful, smelly things. We've been out of toilet paper for a few days and by now have exhausted almost all the tissues, napkins, and paper towels. We are approximately three hours away from resorting to the newspaper or the yellow pages.

Since Saturdays are the time I catch up with all the things that went to hell during the week, I try to wake up early. I pull on my old sweats—just temporarily, but then for the rest of the day I lose awareness of my appearance and end up looking worse at 6:00 P.M. than I did at 6:00 A.M. On my way out, I forget to stop at a mirror and perform the necessary repairs. I look terrible.

The first clue about Saturday-night shopping is the parking lot. The station wagons and minivans that vie for space during the day are replaced by sports cars, Jeeps, and other vehicles that can only comfortably accommodate two people.

When I walk into the store, I notice another difference. People actually look good. They are clean and wear makeup. Their hair conforms to an actual style. Even if they look like they've just been exercising, their sweat looks better than mine. They radiate health, fitness, and self-control.

I wrestle with a shopping cart reluctant to leave its line and begin to walk the programmed maze of the store. A couple in their early thirties are ahead of me. I immediately know that they are single, or at least not married to each other, because they are having too much fun. The store is crowded with this type of people, so it is difficult, despite my well-developed grocery guerrilla tactics, to get around them.

They stop at the fruits-and-vegetables section. Each decision appears to require mutual consent. For me, this is just the place to pick up onions, apples, and two pounds of potatoes. To them it is an exotic jungle. They act like they're picking the stuff off trees. He handles a melon and squeezes it, curving his palm around its contours and raising it to his face to inhale, gazes lasciviously into her eyes, and pronounces it ripe. They indulge in evaluating everything in this Garden of Eden, choosing the most expensive and least durable and practical of the produce.

My fascination with them grows. It's like biting the inside of my cheek where I know it's sore, but I just can't stay away. I'm dying to see what they do next. "You think it's all kiwi and fresh raspberries, don't you?" I mutter to them under my breath. "Yeah, of course it's easy in produce. Fruits and vegetables are sexy. They have exotic colors and shapes. They respond to your touch. They smell delicious. And their taste? God, don't get me started. But let's see how you do with the *rest* of it, when you get to the hard, boring stuff."

They amble down the cheese aisle, leaning together against their cart. The cheese selection is a lot like the fruit selection. As I grab for the package that says "Low-fat processed cheese food," they contemplate the ages of various cheddars, trying to find the perfect match for the fruit in their cart. I'm really getting annoyed with these people. They're too happy. I reach for the least expensive sticks of margarine. They grab a tub of whipped creamery-sweetened butter. I heave two gallons of skim milk into my cart. They choose real cream.

They bypass the deli counter, which is bad, since I am sort of obsessed with them by now, but I still have to buy a pound of thinly sliced boiled ham. I'm lucky; there's no line, so I catch up to them easily. "Just wait for the canned goods," I sneer to myself. "There's nothing like a lot of heavy aluminum cans to weigh a couple down." They turn down the aisle. While I reach for canned tomatoes and applesauce, they delight in discovering canned artichoke hearts and seedless black Italian olives. I didn't even know they *had* those things in that aisle.

It's on to cereal. Guiltily, I grab a box of Count Chocula—the chocolate puffs with little marshmallows that masquerade as breakfast for my daughter. I shake my head, remembering how I conceded that battle much too soon, and how I try to atone for it every day by throwing a Flintstones multivitamin at her. For my husband and me I choose Special K, which is about as close to pure air as a food can get. I defy this couple to find anything to get worked up about in the cereal aisle. She points to a box of something called Muesli, which sounds pretty dreadful. He takes it from the top shelf and reads the box as she describes her skiing trip to Switzerland where she ate it every day mixed with fruit, yogurt, and cream. By the time she finishes, drool has begun to gather at the corner of my mouth. Being the fit and foxy man he is, the guy buys Grape Nuts, the most macho cereal in the aisle, probably because it tastes like eating the gravel from your driveway with milk on it.

Who *are* these people? I obsess. Were my husband and I *ever* like that? I decide that because we married so young and had so little "discretionary" income, grocery shopping was never, for us, an erotic experience.

Choosing the best wine for their meal takes on the import of an international summit. The only thing that doesn't seem to be a factor is cost. He actually says things like "an entertaining little chardonnay" and "a disappointing year." It's hard to tell whether the guy is totally bullshitting the woman, but she looks really impressed. I have to admit that I am too. My husband and I always meant to learn that stuff, but we never did. They search in vain for

Pellegrino water, but to their great dismay they are forced to settle for the rather pedestrian Polar Springs. I throw about ten liters of Diet Coke in my cart as I hear her quoting the dangers of artificial sweeteners.

Each choice they make invites some small celebration. Everything they choose becomes a symbol of an intense, if temporary, commitment to each other. Enough, at least, to get them through a meal.

As I sort through the ground beef, they join the line at the gourmet meat counter, where the pork chops actually have little hats on their ribs. Their choice of veal gives me enormous pleasure, since it's the first time I can feel totally superior to them. What selfish people they are, endorsing the maltreatment of innocent little calves. As I think a little longer, I realize that the ground chuck I'm holding in my hand came from similar brutality, only a bit later.

They bend over the lobster tank. Macho man picks up a pegged lobster and teases her with it, flashing it in her naturally made-up face. She responds like she's five years old, with exaggerated fear and revulsion. I want to ram her cart and say, "You think *that's* scary, honey? It's *nothing*. Just wait till you get to the aisle packed with diapers and rectal baby thermometers, not to mention all the stuff for when your bowels can't move and your bladder can't stop."

I can no longer pretend that I'm behind these people by some stroke of fate. I am stalking them. And I can't give them up. I follow them into aisles where I have no business. I can't help the way I stare as they choose coffee. They inhale the Hazelnut Decafe as if it were marijuana, and give a similar look of satisfaction upon exhaling.

We head into the homestretch: frozen foods—the final test. The aisle where I buy at least a quarter of my groceries—microwave pancakes and pizzas, low-calorie meals that I swear to eat exclusively and don't, bags of vegetables, maybe a turkey breast. They go straight for ice creams, arguing the merits of Ben and Jerry's versus Häagen-Dazs. I'm thankful for the absence of sampling tables, knowing that watching these two feed each other double-chocolate-fudge-chunk ice cream would be more than my poor heart could bear.

No longer do I want to ram their cart. Now I want to hijack it. In a moment when they are caught up in some sexual culinary encounter, I want to sidle up to their cart and commandeer it. I want to ingest their lives. To swallow them whole so that my husband and I might become them for at least one meal. And, by leaving them my cart, I will provide them with a valuable taste of real life. Let *them* struggle with coupons and rebates. Let *them* listen to, "You *know* I hate that," or "God, we're having *that* again? Why can't we ever have . . . ?"

I want to surprise my husband with their food. We will unpack their bags together, running our hands over the produce, relishing the richness of the meat, the promise of expensive champagne. Our daughter will hear our rapid breathing and see the heat rise in our cheeks. She will demand to know what's going on, since she's never seen us this happy in the kitchen before. And we will smile and pretend not to know what she's saying. As I watch my husband inhale the raspberries, I will forgive him for letting me become careless with myself and him. And he will forgive me for forgetting the toilet paper.

Last Rites

Here I go

I divested myself of despair
and fear when I came here.
Now there is no more catching
one's own eye in the mirror,
there are no bad books, no plastic,
no insurance premiums, and of course
no illness. Contrition
does not exist, nor gnashing
of teeth. No one howls as the first
clod of dirt hits the casket.
The poor we no longer have with us.
Our calm hearts strike only the hour,
and God, as promised, proves
to be mercy clothed in light.

—Jane Kenyon,
   "Notes from the Other Side"

🌿 HANDS

DYING WOMEN have beautiful hands. It's a beauty that never comes from trying.

Their hands are no longer manicured or polished. Life's too short for that. Hands are reservoirs, the last stop a life makes before its leaving. Bodies waste away. But hands prevail. Cherished rings slide up and down with the movement of slender fingers. With the slow motion of effort and agony, each tiny bone, each fold of skin, once imperceptible, now is magnified.

My dying patient's hands do little but point and pray and wait. They are riveting as they lift and fall on flowered sheets, casting swan shadows on the wall. They reach in love, grip in fear, wrench in pain, and finally, rest mercifully in sleep. My arm hangs over her bed rail, aching after only minutes. I miss the old power of my words. Now, only my hands can help. Smoothing her hair, tilting her water glass, stroking her face. Finally, her breathing deepens. She quiets. Our hands move together in her sleep.

I study my hand, folded over hers, as it rises and falls against her chest. My hands are disappointments. The skin is rough and coarse, as if I spend my time outdoors in hard labor. The nails are broken and jagged, all varieties of shapes and lengths. My attempts at show are failures. In bursts of femininity, I file and paint them. But the polish never gets completely on or comes completely off. Each finger has its own war story, its own excuse for ugliness. They work too long in dirt and dishwater. They are callused by bad handwriting that the nuns never could correct. There is always one with a wrinkled, waterlogged Band-Aid from careless burns or bramble scratches.

My hands have no patience. My face can mask anxiety, but my hands will never lie. They worry and wring. They drum to protest wasted time. They emphasize points, they threaten bad children, they salute cars that cut me off in traffic. They beat egg whites and sort socks. They dance on computer keyboards and scrub the toilets.

But my hands were meant for more than work. They beat and bounce on steering wheels and tabletops when music defies me to be still. They raise themselves in victory at a point scored or something just turning out right. They savor the textures of living—the softness of my daughter's fair skin, the curve of my husband's strong calves, the grip of a knife handle as I slice into a ripe melon. My hands have learned to comfort, entice, tickle, and tease, discovering just the right places to give and know joy.

These hands have never known how to *look*, but they've started learning how to live. I am happily resigned to nails too short and cuticles too long. Despite my best intentions, my hands will revert to sandpaper. But it's all right. My hands look bad, but they serve me rather well.

For once in my life, I celebrate my ordinariness.

My hands are not beautiful.

I am not dying.

❧ SNOW ANGELS

SNOW IS NOT the same anymore. Once it was a gift, each flake its own separate miracle. Cold the consistency of confectioners' sugar, it was sweet to the taste as we tilted our heads and stuck out our tongues to receive communion from the clouds. Snow was silence and stillness. It evened out the edges and made the ugliness disappear. The most scorching summer day couldn't approach the brilliance of fresh snow in a new morning's sun.

Each snowfall awakened us with giddiness at its white magic. We nudged each other from sleep to witness the evening's handiwork and to celebrate the holiday that it guaranteed. In our neighborhood it was important to be the first ones out, beating even the paperboy in planting our footprints on the perfect snow.

Although we were treading upon the same spots we had traversed hundreds of times before, somehow our steps on new snow felt courageous and special. To make the first footprint, despite the fact that you were just a plain old kid leaving a size-five boot mark, was to establish yourself on land that was totally indifferent and unyielding to you at any other time.

In our large family, for purposes of convenience and symmetry the six children were divided into two groups: the "big kids" and the "little kids." Membership in the "bigs" meant greater freedom, but with it, the resented responsibility of looking out for the "littles."

With a new snow, the big kids slipped silently from bed, sneaking past the rooms of little kids who would beg to tag along and parents who would demand things like breakfast and chores. Chip, Sarah, and I tiptoed down to the basement and rifled through the baskets of snow clothes and boots. We positioned ourselves on the concrete floor in size order—an assembly line of sorts, in which we tried on jackets, boots, and snow pants. If they fit, you kept them; if not, they moved on down the line. We covered our shoes with plastic bread bags held up with rubber bands in preparation for the most difficult task, putting on our boots. Dressing for snow often meant packing loose boots with extra socks or mittens or lying on your back and having your siblings force you into boots that were a size too small, a procedure that was much more likely to lead to injury than any trouble you could possibly find outside.

Just when we were ready to go, smug in our solidarity, we would hear the voice of the person we were always most intent on eluding—Priscilla. Priscilla was the biggest of the little kids. Her sole mission in life was the statistically impossible task of becoming one of the big kids. She could hear the softest steps pass her door. One creaking plank, one loud whisper, and she was out of bed, sniffing around for action. She would run downstairs half-dressed in some ridiculous outfit, pronouncing herself ready to join us. It was always a tradeoff at this point—stand there sweating in layers of snow clothes and run the risk of being nailed by parents or beaten to the punch by other kids, or give in to Priscilla. In the end it was always easier to throw some clothes on her and allow her to tag along. Zipped into her one-piece snowsuit with its puffy hood and snap-on mittens, she looked more like an astronaut than a five-year-old. Her balance on flat surfaces in all that gear was tenuous. I realized in frustration that it would only be worse in snow.

Sometimes it took all three of us to push open the back door through a pile of drifted snow. We were like prisoners at the moment of escape, forcing the door open a crack, pulling it back, inching farther and farther until we could finally squeeze our bodies through the opening. Once outside, Chip and Sarah ran free, littering the backyard with their footprints. But it was always I, the biggest of the big kids, who was left to deal with Priscilla. Priscilla did not move easily in snow. It often reached her thighs, and she was as likely to fall over to her left or her right as she was to remain vertical. She had no sense of depth and quickly succumbed to snowdrifts as if they were quicksand, always sputtering and calling out my name.

I loved to march through the snow with strong, solitary, crunching steps, taking great delight in the evidence of my trail. Priscilla always tried to follow, yelling, "Wait up, Martha. Wait up!" She alternated between calling my name and falling like a drunkard every few steps.

"Priscilla," I yelled at her, "watch out for my footsteps. Put your feet in them."

"I can't," she wailed.

"Yes, you can. One foot, then the other. Hurry up or I'll leave you."

Under that kind of pressure she quickly established the rhythm of the march and was thrilled that she was following my path so precisely. "Martha. We're having a parade!" she sang. Looking back at her struggling through the snow, her cheeks already bright red, her breath visible from such concerted effort, I shook my head, rolling my eyes at no one in particular.

By now Chip and Sarah had circled around to the front yard, where they were busy staking out territory for snow angels. Making a snow angel involves an act of faith on the part of any child. One learns that the snow is like water: you can close your eyes, loosen your body, fall back, and the snow will catch you and hold you gently if you let it. Unlike water, which quickly closes ranks and erases all evidence of your fall, snow yields to the body, leaving an impression that lasts, at least for a while. Snow angels are made by falling backward. You allow your head to rest still, and your arms and legs to do horizontal jumping jacks, moving the snow back and forth like the windshield wipers on a car. Back and forth you move until you're sure you've made a deep enough impression. Then you stand up very carefully so you don't mar your creation before you've had a chance to admire it.

And if you haven't screwed up too badly, what you have to admire is a thing of beauty. These are not the cherubic little angels who buzz around the saints or hang out with Cupid. They are not the well-meaning guardian angels who perch atop children's beds or night-lights. These are archangels. The big guns. They are angels of substance and strength. They preside over Christmas trees. They protect and defend, promising refuge under their magnificent outstretched wings. If you're in a jam, these are the angels you want to call.

I claimed a piece of ground that Chip and Sarah had somehow left unsullied, loosened my body, closed my eyes, and fell. As I fell back, Priscilla did too.

But as I was delighting in swinging my arms and legs up and down, Priscilla was drowning in snow. She kicked and cried, her little red boots protesting in the air, the top of a tiny green mitten signaling for help. Each time she tried to copy my movements, she covered herself with more snow. I ran over and scooped her out of the hole she had created for herself. She fought me all the time, furious that she couldn't leave an impression like mine. Her teeth were chattering, her nose was running, and her lips were turning blue, but she refused to go in without making a snow angel. I lifted her up and laid her in the snow angel I had made. She swung her arms and legs up and down, safe in the place that my larger body had created for her.

When she was fully satisfied, I lifted her from the arms of the angel and stood her up in front of me. She had not made much of an impression on the snow, but the snow had made a tremendous impression on her. It was so thick that it obscured the colors of her snowsuit, boots, and mittens. It was matted in her hair and lingered on her nose and lips as if she had inhaled it. I tried to brush her off, but it was like beating a rug that has no intention of giving up its dust. She resisted my efforts and demanded that she be allowed to keep the snow. I was tired of her and the cold, so I didn't press the point. I gave up and turned to lead her back to the house. This time she automatically stepped in my footsteps and remained vertical and triumphant for the entire walk back. I checked behind me at the freezing cold, scrappy kid who sang out loud as she tramped through the deep snow and I realized that I envied her. She may not have been a big kid, but she already knew something that I didn't. Priscilla knew how to be so happy on so very little.

We are all grown-ups now, and snow is not the same. To our children, snow is still a white wonder to be claimed and celebrated. To us it is an impediment, an obstacle to be overcome. The gifts of school holidays are now complications in our child-care schedules. We know now how brief the snow stays pure and white and how long it lingers in piles along roads and paths, turning gray and stubborn, resisting even a sunny day that invites it to disappear.

Chasing Grace

Priscilla's husband died on a snowy day. In the space between breaths, his heart went on strike—totally resistant to any negotiation with the massive technology called in to save him. He was much too young for that. But it happened anyway.

Death in a family is such a shattering, incomprehensible event that it is easy to imagine everyone sitting for days wailing, screaming, or totally withdrawing into sorrow. The irony is that at the very moment when life loses its order, its center, we are expected to spring into incredibly organized action.

As we sat around Priscilla's living room, we made lists and assigned chores, in much the same way we had as children. "Martha, you write the eulogy. Rachel, you take care of the printing. Mark, call the caterer. Sarah, talk to the priest. Chip, you go with Priscilla and Mom and Dad to the funeral home." People dispersed singly or in groups to carry out their missions. And in that process we tried to reconcile the everyday motions of starting a car and finding a parking space, of ordering food and flowers, of arranging for baby-sitters and answering the phone with the fact that the entire world was going on while our brother-in-law lay dead. How many people in how many cars were going about ordinary business in similar extraordinary situations? I read the obituary section of the local newspaper and counted the number of entries, multiplying the number of people in my family by all the names on the list. And I cried and held the paper close to me, embracing them all as they left their imprints on my white silk blouse.

In an amazingly short time, we completed our chores—all except the most difficult, the choice of a gravesite. We slushed through the snow in long leather boots and dark coats, following the cemetery salesman. From gravesite to gravesite we walked and then stood back so that Priscilla could evaluate each. Her criteria for selection was never really articulated, and even the salesman didn't have the nerve to ask her what exactly she had in mind. It was almost as if not choosing a plot might delay the inevitable. The last cemetery was the smallest and simplest. The caretaker pointed out the possibilities and we walked back and forth in a small parade. She kept returning to one in particular. It was on a hill next to the grave of a young child who had died recently.

That seemed to be some comfort to Priscilla, but still she couldn't make a final decision. We stood silently in a semicircle around the gravesite, knowing that only Priscilla could make the choice. She handed her large black purse to my mother and took several steps closer to the place where the headstone would be placed. And then she lay down on her back in the snow. Her arms were spread out at her sides, and I half expected her to move her arms and legs to make a snow angel. But she didn't. She crossed her hands over her chest and lay silently in the snow, in the position in which her husband would lie in his casket. She turned her head to the right, to the left, craned her neck to see behind her and then looked straight ahead. And then for a moment she closed her eyes and lay completely still. We watched in silence as my sister made her peace with the place where her husband would rest. Priscilla's husband's heart had broken, and one by one, I could almost hear the shattering of the hearts around me, hidden by faces trying so hard to be stoic.

Priscilla nodded her head and we knew that she had made her choice. As she began to stand, I reached out a hand to steady and help her up. In those few seconds, she was five again and I was eleven, pulling her up as she looked back to admire her impression in the snow. Now we all looked at the imprint of her body, knowing that in twenty-four hours that place would hold her husband.

The back of her plum-colored coat was completely covered with snow. But unlike old times, no one rushed to brush it off. In some gift of wisdom we knew enough to let those flakes melt into her and connect her always to the place where her husband would rest. Priscilla turned and headed toward the car, creating fresh footprints with every step as we walked behind her.

Now Priscilla is the big kid. I follow as she makes her way through the long cold snow ahead. And I let myself imagine, just for a moment, that one of those magnificent snow angels of our childhood will protect us all from getting lost in the drifts.

❧ IRISH WAKE

MY FIRST IRISH WAKE was also my last. It was my first wake of any kind, the first time I had seen a person laid out in a coffin—dead. One of my father's aunts had died. An aunt I didn't know. All I knew was that we were going to stop at her house on the way from Boston to New York. I had no idea that *she* was going to be there.

The talking and laughing I heard as I stepped into the front hallway were not the hushed and somber sounds I expected in a house in which a family member had died. Closer to the kitchen, it even looked like a party—a big one. People were drinking. Red-faced men with broad Boston accents smoked cigars, threw back whiskey, and regaled one another with expansive stories. I asked my mother if she was sure we were in the right house. I'd never dealt with death, but I expected black clothes, pale faces, and a great deal of crying. These people were laughing. What could possibly be funny at a time like this?

My father disappeared among his relatives, many of whom he hadn't seen for years. My younger brother and sisters were sent immediately up the long, curving staircase to a room where a baby-sitter was minding children. My brother Chip and I, who had changed into our good clothes at a rest stop, didn't know what was expected of us. My mother was deep in conversation with several women. When I tapped her on the shoulder and asked what Chip and I were supposed to do, she looked around, saw that there were no other kids, and told us we could run upstairs with the other children. "But first," she said, "go see your aunt." We looked confused. We had a lot of aunts. One of the women talking with my mother volunteered, "I'll take them."

We followed behind her, keeping close watch as we threaded through clusters of people, on the lookout for any of our aunts. The woman, who finally introduced herself as Eileen, one of my father's first cousins, led us down a quieter hallway. She rounded a corner and entered the first room on the right. From the angle where I was standing, I could see only long candles in huge brass candlesticks, just like in church. But one second later, she stepped to her left and ushered us into the room. "Here's Aunt Margaret," she said, as if she were introducing her on a TV game show. Aunt Margaret was laid out in a coffin, in a regular room. There were church kneelers at the coffin and floral arrangements everywhere. My father's cousin said, "Don't you think she looks good?" I didn't have the heart or the guts to ask her if she meant "looks good for a dead person" or "looks good for Aunt Margaret." Since I had no basis of comparison for either judgment, I re-mained silent. My brother Chip was so pale that his freckles looked ready to jump off his face.

Aunt Margaret was dressed in a pale rose nightgown and a chiffon robe. Her arms were folded across her chest, and the rosary beads in her hand made it look like she was praying. In-tently. I wondered how they got the rosary beads around hands that looked so stiff. My brother and I knelt down, blessed our-selves, and tried to pray. I should have prayed for Aunt Margaret's soul, but my biggest concern at the moment was not throwing up. My brother whispered to me that the whole thing was "disgust-ing." It was way past disgusting for me. It was unthinkable that you could just park a dead person in a house, even if it *was* hers. How could the rest of her family not have a terminal sense of the creeps? And how could people party in one room with a dead person under the same roof? How could they digest ham sandwiches and potato salad on top of that knowledge? How could they drink? And what in God's name was there to laugh about?

Chip and I bolted upstairs as fast as we could. We found the room with the kids and were happy to see some of our cousins, who seemed much more sophisticated about the whole thing. When I confided to my older cousin about how disgusting I thought it all was, she said, "Get used to it. It's a typical Irish wake."

I retorted, "Well, I don't have to get used to it because I'm not Irish."

My cousin looked at me impatiently and insisted, "Of course you're Irish: half the people here are O'Neills. You are an O'Neill."

Until that point, I'd considered myself a "Yankee." My mother's great-grandfather was a Hale, a New England Yankee, breaking a long streak of pure Irish Catholic blood. He was a Northern Baptist, an anomaly in the generations. But he was so loved by his children and grandchildren that their identification was always with him and "his people." I knew that our family was very Catholic, but no one had ever mentioned anything about Irish. Once my cousin convinced me that we were, in fact, Irish, I shuddered in anticipation of all the wakes in front of me.

As we watched TV and talked, we could hear the volume downstairs increase as the liquor bottles emptied. Pretty soon, people were getting stupid, making their kids perform in those awful dog-and-pony shows where children with the tiniest bit of talent are forced to display it publicly in front of a bunch of slobbering grown-ups. Fortunately for me, I had no discernible talent and was spared. Chip, however, had been playing guitar for several years. My father, who'd had a few too many, told him to get his guitar and sing for everyone. My brother refused. My father insisted. Chip sputtered and got his ten-year-old butt out to the car to get his guitar.

He sat down amid comments in the background of "Isn't he adorable?" and "He's John and Mary Lou's second." Chip waited for several seconds for quiet and then somehow sensed that this venue would be more like playing in a bar than a living room. The sooner he started playing, the sooner it would be over. Everyone pressed around as my brother, the altar boy, the freckle-faced, crew-cut kid in the navy blazer, gray slacks, white shirt, and little red bow tie, chose a song appropriate to the occasion. He strummed a few bars and then sang out mournfully, "There is . . . a house . . . in New Orleeeaaanns. They calllll . . . the Risin' Sun. And it's been . . . the ruin . . . of many a poor boy, . . . and God, . . . I know . . . I'm one . . ." He really belted it out. Somehow, I don't think a song about a whorehouse was exactly what my father had in mind. But Chip sang it with such a straight face, I'm sure my father assumed my brother didn't know what he was singing. He may have been right. All I remember is that my parents cleared their throats and looked down at the floor a lot. People clapped politely when he was finished and no encores were requested.

On the way back to New York, I was vocal in my distress. I told my mother that wakes were disgraceful. Wakes at *home* were even worse. And wakes at home with *drinking and laughing* were unforgivable. I told her that I thought it was terrible that people acted so happy, as if Aunt Margaret hadn't died. She explained that if I'd seen everyone before the wake, and if we had stayed for the funeral, we would have seen many tears. Then she tried to tell me how death wasn't such a bad thing. "In death," she said, "people are called by God to a new life and that is something to celebrate." Her explanation was of no comfort. "But why have it at home?" I insisted. She told me that Aunt Margaret's wake was done the "old way" but that most wakes were held at funeral parlors. "Why do they have to leave that long box open? Who wants to see a dead person?" My mother answered that it helps people have some time to get used to the person they love being dead. And it lets them remember the dead person at peace. Then I asked a lot of technical questions, basically from the worms-go-in, worms-go-out line of childhood inquiry—embalming, preservation, rigor mortis. What happened if they made a mistake and the person wasn't really dead? There were nights back home when I had nightmares about dead Aunt Margaret. Sometimes I couldn't go to sleep because I kept thinking about dead bodies, especially my own.

By the time I reached adolescence, more people I knew were dying. My parents' relatives, their friends' relatives, a priest or a nun here and there, even some children. Wakes weren't held at people's homes. They were at funeral parlors where you went for "viewings." Funeral homes were dark, somber places with ugly carpeting, few windows, and furniture that went out of its way to be nondescript. Just as in hotels where they had signs for events— "Tyler wedding in the Ambassador ballroom"—funeral homes posted the dead people's names and room numbers. You could easily get lost in these "homes." Usually several wakes were scheduled simultaneously. If you made a wrong turn, you could end up offering your condolences to the wrong people. There was always a room with a casket and hardly any mourners. Sometimes I was more taken by the person in that room than the person I was supposed to see. Why was she so alone? Had her life been as lonely as the body in that room? Or had she lived a life so good that she just outlasted everyone else?

I always seemed to get dragged to wakes of popular people. The rooms were packed, and the smell of flowers, sweat, breath, old-lady perfume, and grief was overwhelming. I felt enormous pressure to think of appropriate things to say. I had most of the ritual down: You had to get in line for the casket, kneel down, and make the sign of the cross. Then you were supposed to pray for God to have mercy on the soul of the "dearly departed." But I was always so self-conscious that I just closed my eyes, bent my head, and obsessed, *Is this long enough? I can't stand it. Would it be okay if I got up now? Do I look like I'm praying?* I'd always be there just in time to get stuck in that airless room when Father Whoever made his perfunctory visit, which almost always culminated in the full recitation of the rosary. He'd say the first part of each prayer. The mourners would say the second. After a while it was like white noise—I had to work to keep from closing my eyes, swaying, and falling asleep. At the end of the wake, we were always handed a holy card with a picture of Jesus or Mary, a prayer on the back, the dead person's name and date of death engraved in black or gold—and the name of the funeral home. They had the good taste not to print their phone number.

The last few people in my life who have died have been considerably closer to me than the people in my childhood, a trend that will sadly increase with time. In the most recent and painful deaths, my reaction to wakes has come full circle, back to Aunt Margaret. When my brother-in-law died suddenly at the age of forty-four, his wake was held at a funeral home. It was scheduled for two hours, from 7:00 to 9:00 P.M. At 9:15, the funeral-home managers began to shepherd us out. If I had been my sister, I would have totally lost it at that moment. I would have screamed, "Don't you dare tell me I have to leave my husband in cold storage in this place to spend the night with other dead people. Two days ago, this man was laughing. He was reading the newspaper. He was hugging me hard. My time with him is not up yet. I know it will be soon. But not yet." They will think I am falling apart, but they will be wrong. I will be in full possession of whatever faculties I have left, knowing best how I need to mourn.

Now, when someone I love dies, I can't imagine having the wake anywhere but at home. I don't foresee a quiet, somber house anymore, either. Now I understand the eating and the drinking, the talking and even the laughing. I understand that they were never *substitutes* for grieving. They were *part* of grieving. In the middle of experiencing acute grief, you have to take some breaks or it will kill you too.

When I think of my husband, I understand why my Aunt Margaret was "laid out" at home. I want him with me until the absolute last moment I have to give him up. Those hours between his final breath and his burial will help me mark his transition from life to death. I don't mean the exact point at which his heart stops beating and someone records the time on a death certificate. I mean the process by which his soul passes from his body and travels to someplace else. I want to witness that passage. I want to sit vigil through the night, taking turns keeping watch with other people who love him. I will lay my head on his hands and cry. I will slam my fists against the casket in rage. I will chuckle sitting there alone with my husband, wondering what absurd comment he would make if he were there. And I will stroke his face and talk to him about our life, filling in the gaps of things I should have said and taking back some of the things I shouldn't have.

In death, as in life, we will be Irish—surrounded by our friends and family, by the music we love, by grand stories inflated with every telling, by drinking and eating (in that order), by the free flow of tears, and by one of the greatest comforts in grief: a couple of straight shots of laughter.

❧ GOLDFISH

I AM BY PROFESSION a psychologist. One might assume that this enhances my ability as a mother. It does not. In fact, it is more often an impediment than an aid. My assumption is that exploring feelings and sharing those feelings with loved ones is the way to live an enlightened life. But things get complicated when one's child does not share this conviction—and from birth wages active resistance against it.

Martha Manning

I should have known it with the goldfish when she was just four years old. All the signs were there. Her goldfish, Harvard and San Diego, were, as she often lamented, "the closest I'll ever get to having pets." Keara was a mastermind at guilt and it was never wasted on her mother, who was allergic to all fur-bearing animals.

At the pet store, she stood for an eternity surveying the goldfish, offering personality analyses of each. The fish all looked the same to me, but not to her. "She looks like a brat." "This one's too shy." She finally picked the two she determined had the most lively "personalities." But it didn't end there. The goldfish trade had become considerably more complicated than when I was a child. In addition to the necessities of a bowl and a net, there were special fish-food flakes, dechlorination drops, algae, special rocks, and even fish toys. I assented to everything but the fish toys until Keara delivered the zinger, "Mom, they'll get lonely too while you're out working." More guilt. It worked. The fish got their toys.

Harvard and San Diego moved into her room with great ceremony and excitement. But after less than thirty minutes of intent goldfish watching, she didn't find them all that interesting. In fact, by the end of the day, I wished we had just rented them, like videos that can only be kept overnight.

Instead of teaching my child to be responsible, having goldfish taught me how to be responsible for my child. Initially, I was quite diligent in caring for her pets, or as she continued to call them, her "almost pets." But after a while, even I became lax. Sitting at dinner, I'd get a twinge and ask urgently, "Has anyone fed the goldfish lately?" With that, one of us would gasp, run upstairs, and give them a sprinkle of fish-food flakes.

Their bowl became grungier with time, with my husband and I waging silent standoffs about whose turn it was to clean it. When Keara's room began to smell like a swamp, one of us broke down and lugged the bowl to the kitchen sink, all the while lamenting the general lack of responsibility in our household. Then came the weekly disagreement about whose idea it was to get the "damn goldfish," as they were affectionately called, in the first place. Somehow Keara always managed to extricate herself from the whole mess, quite content to let her father and me battle it out.

I'll never forget that day. "D-Day," my husband calls it. It was Thanksgiving. The kind of cold, dark, New England day that helps you understand why the pilgrims almost didn't make it. We were expected at relatives' in the early afternoon and spent the morning catching up with the week's dirty rooms, dishes, and laundry. When I came close to Keara's room, the smell and the crud on the bowl told me there was no escaping it—the bowl had to be cleaned. But I was distracted. It had been a tough week— too much work, difficult patients. But I'm making excuses again. After all these years, I still feel bad about what I did. This guilt is reinforced constantly by a family that won't let me forget.

Things started out well. I scrubbed the bowl and changed the water. It sounds easy, but it isn't. Those little fish were always tough to get back into their bowl. One of them usually ended up flipping out of the net and panicking on the kitchen floor. And goldfish aren't easy to retrieve when they're upset. In retrospect, they actually had some cause for concern. As I scooped San Diego off the floor, I tried to reassure him in my best psychologist's voice, which had about as much impact on the fish as it ever did on my child.

We were doing fine until we got to the dechlorinating part. Anyone who's owned goldfish knows that tap water is not good for them and that several drops of chemicals must be added to rid the water of chlorine. Unfortunately, this proved to be one of those cases in which there actually can be too much of a good thing.

The phone rang as I was placing the drops in the bowl, and from what we could piece together later, I must have put a couple too many drops in. I scooped the fish back into the bowl and continued to talk on the phone. In no more than five seconds, they shot to the top of the bowl, turned side up, and floated rigidly in their extraordinarily clean water.

"Oh no! The goldfish! I have to hang up!"

I yelled for my husband to come quickly.

I pointed to the bowl.

"What did you do to the goldfish?"

"I don't know," I answered. "Do you think they're dead?"

"No, I think they're doing the sidestroke. Of course they're dead. How did you do that?"

"Would you keep your voice down," I hissed between clenched teeth. "I don't know; maybe I put too many drops in. Anyway, it was *your* turn," I said, trying to share the burden of guilt. "How are we going to tell her?"

"What do you mean, *we?* You did it. You tell her."

She was watching *Sesame Street,* sitting cross-legged on the family-room couch.

"Hi, Sweetie. I have some bad news . . . Harvard and San Diego aren't alive anymore."

"You mean they're dead?"

"Well, yeah, pretty much." I was having a hard time being direct. Her trusting blue eyes had filled with enormous tears that were beginning a torturously slow descent down her cheeks.

"Something happened while I was cleaning their bowl, maybe too many drops. You see too many chemicals can . . ." I hoped a scientific explanation might gain us some distance from the pain.

"Oh no," she wailed. "I'll miss them so much."

"Honey, would you please stop saying that. I'll get you more tomorrow. First thing. I promise."

She put her head down against the couch and started to cry.

"Keara, is there anything I can do for you?" I whispered as I put my arm around her.

"Yeah," she sniffed. "Leave me alone."

I can't remember too many times when I've felt like a worse mother. Not only was I the perpetrator of my child's pain, I was totally inept in comforting her about it.

What could I do with all this distress? I searched for ways to salvage the unfortunate situation. Then it came to me. This was actually a golden moment, an opportunity to teach one of life's great lessons, to share something of great significance with my child. I would transform this awful mistake into something good. We would have a funeral. A goldfish funeral for the dearly departed Harvard and San Diego. My husband suggested a "burial at sea": a couple of kind words, a flush, and that would be that. I could not believe his callousness. Plus, I reasoned, flushing dead things would be confusing to a child of this age.

It was time to teach her about death, about the observance of loss, and about getting on with life. I began to get really enthusiastic about the funeral idea. I figured we could obtain a lot of mileage out of these goldfish. I began to feel less helpless, even optimistic that I could convert this random accident into an important family milestone.

I quickly prepared the service in my head. We would each say a few words about the fish and bury them under the deck in the backyard. I found a small plastic bag and scooped the fish out of the bowl. My garden tools were packed away for the winter, so I grabbed an old fork to use for digging the hole. I called everyone to come outside.

That was when the trouble started.

Keara yelled down, "Oh, Mom, it's too cold and *Sesame Street* isn't over yet."

My husband echoed her resistance, warning, "You do remember, don't you, that we are expected at dinner in an hour."

I was undaunted. "Come on. This will only take a minute. It's important."

We pulled on our coats and went to the backyard. It had begun to sleet, and even I found it terribly cold. I carried the bag with reverence and ceremony. Solemnly, I asked my daughter to choose a spot. She pointed halfheartedly to a spot on the ground and added, "This is really gross."

We stood silently for a moment. Then I asked her if she'd like to say any final words. She looked down for a moment, so I assumed she was collecting her thoughts. I was ready to be moved. Then she shrugged casually and said, "No, not really."

"Well, can't you think of *something?*" I prompted.

"Like what?"

"Like how they were good goldfish. Like how you liked having them in your room. Like how you'll miss them."

"Yeah, Mom. That's good."

"No, honey, they were *your* goldfish. I thought you might want to say something in your own words." I was beginning to grit my teeth and the tone of my voice sounded more like a command than a suggestion. "What would *you* like to say?"

"What I would like to say is, Mom, how much longer is this going to take?"

My husband pointed to the sleet and remarked again about the time and the cold.

At that point I could have easily added them to the day's killing spree.

"Listen, we're going to bury these damn goldfish, so you might as well participate." I bent down and struck the rocky soil with my little fork. It was New England November frozen solid. I tried again . . . and again. The fork was no match for the ground and began to bend. A couple of bits of dirt loosened. I struck harder. Even in the cold, I was working up a sweat. I looked up from my crouch to see my husband and daughter staring at me as if I were an alien. This made me angrier, and I stabbed the ground even harder. Every few stabs, I laid the little bag in the indentation of earth I'd made to see if it was deep enough.

Keara piped up, "Mom, you're going to have to go much deeper than that."

"Did it ever occur to the two of you that you might help?"

"But there's only one fork," they replied lamely.

I loosened more dirt and ground the bag into what could only optimistically be called a hole. Then I collected rocks to cover what the dirt didn't. I stood up holding my battered fork and began the service, "Everything has a beginning and an end. Some things live a very long time. And other things live a very short time. This is what life is all about. *It's nobody's fault.* Sometimes life . . . "

"Mom," Keara cut me short, "I'm shivering. Can I please go in?"

"Yes, go in. Go ahead, both of you. Go in and ruin this whole thing," I whined in my best martyr voice, which was totally wasted on them. They were halfway to the house when, over her shoulder, Keara finally offered her send-off to the deceased, "Bye, guys." That was as close to a benediction as the child was going to get.

I stood alone, in the cold, with the buried fish. Little pieces of bag stuck out from the rocks and the dirt. But it was getting late. This clearly had not gone the way I had hoped. I needed to cut my losses and bring the ceremony to a close.

"Well, guys, I'm really sorry it came to this. You know I didn't mean it."

I was talking to dead goldfish, half hoping one would offer absolution from the grave. Slowly it became evident to me that this was just another mistake I would have to tolerate. I gave a heavy sigh and walked into the house, thinking about how things always worked out better in the movies or on television or in other people's families.

We bought more goldfish. This time it took only two minutes to pick them out.

She didn't give a thought to the names. She just called them Harvard and San Diego again. They took up residence in her room, and she seemed to adjust to the loss quite well. It took some time for me to recover from a serious case of bowl-cleaning phobia, especially with my husband and daughter joining in with the theme song from the movie *Jaws*, with one of them always leering, "Just when you thought it was safe to be a goldfish . . ." Within two weeks, I recovered my sense of humor and felt renewed confidence in my capacity to care for fish.

Several weeks later, I went to pick up Keara from her preschool. As I climbed the stairs, I noticed signs announcing "Dr. Martha Manning's talk on children's social development," a presentation I had agreed to months before that was scheduled for later in the week. Lining the hall walls were brand-new projects the children had done on the theme "Feelings."

The title of these paintings was "The Saddest Thing . . ." I was touched by the children's paintings, already calculating how I could integrate them into my talk that week. Then I stopped in horror at Keara's. Despite her rudimentary drawing skills, the picture was unmistakable. Two dead goldfish floated at the top of a bowl of water. Above her picture were Keara's words, dictated to a teacher and printed in big, bold, black letters:

THE SADDEST THING . . . WAS WHEN MY MOM KILLED MY GOLDFISH!

Her name was written under it in huge letters. Two horrible scenes immediately flashed in front of me. The first was the picture of Dr. Martha "Bad Mother" Manning addressing the parents of the preschoolers later that week. The second scenario involved Keara, sometime in the future, on a therapist's couch working through her hostility at her fish-murdering mother.

Bad-mother mistakes never die. They take on a life of their own. They will never be forgotten. Bad-mother mistakes are inevitable.

And the scary part is that I am making some now, probably at this very moment, without even knowing it. But she will know. And someday she will tell her friends or perfect strangers, or maybe even me in an angry moment. And I will be as puzzled as my mother looks each time I say accusingly, "Remember the time you . . ."

So in the meantime, I just do the best I can. I feed the fish when I remember. I clean the bowl when it can't be avoided. And no matter what else, I always count the dechlorination drops.

❧ LAST WILL AND TESTAMENT

Upon my impending death, please read the following and comply as fully as possible.

Dying is bad enough. The combination of death and pain is unacceptable. Force the doctors to give me as many painkillers as it takes. Given the addictive branches of my family tree, I have heretofore been vigilant about avoiding dependence on drugs. But if I'm already dying, screw it. I want drugs—lots of them. Score them on the street if you have to.

Immediately post mortem, my husband (or closest living friend) is to empty my bedside drawer of the two vibrators, three Anaïs Nin books, and twelve sets of rosary beads. No one would understand.

I want a simple wake. Most people say they want to be buried in a plain wooden box. But somehow, when their families are vulnerable in loss, the death merchants make them feel cheap if they don't buy mahogany and brass, guaranteed waterproof. I mean it: I want a plain wooden box, like those the monks use to bury their brothers. Use the money you saved on a totally impractical car. Landscape the house with gorgeous flowers. Give the money to a poor man on the street. Whatever you choose, I promise that you'll get a lot more mileage out of it than I'll get out of a casket.

Don't let them put makeup on me and do weird stuff to my hair. Let me look as shitty as I did when I died. It will help people believe that I'm better off dead.

Don't dress me up. I'm going to have to spend a long time in those clothes. I recommend my navy sweatpants with my hooded gray sweatshirt, or my plaid flannel nightgown.

If anyone says, "She looks like she's sleeping," eject him or her forcefully from the room.

Do not allow carnations or gladioli anywhere near me.

At my wake, play the music I've always loved in the background. No "easy listening," which is just a euphemism for elevator music. Music shouldn't be easy. Just because I'm knocked out doesn't mean everyone else has to be. You can't go wrong with Motown, Puccini, or any woman with the earth in her voice. For my funeral I would like the Magnificat (in Latin), "I Don't Feel No Ways Tired," and "Precious Lord."

Don't mourn me politely. Make a huge scene. You'll feel better.

Don't leave me alone in the funeral home. I get frightened around dead people.

My daughter is to receive all my published and unpublished writing. I have separated the unpublished manuscripts and journals into specific decades or events in her life. I have reserved writing for her forties that she couldn't possibly appreciate in her twenties. There is a collection for when she gets married, for when she becomes a mother, for when she begins to lose heart, for her great successes, for her lowest moments. I will leave it to her to decide the appropriate time to open each box. I would ask that she be gentle with me as she reads the words I have left behind. They were never meant as words of wisdom, only as markers of my particular journeys.

The following document is to be given to my daughter upon my death.

As you know, the women in my family live to be very old and fairly cranky, which your father always said was fine, since the men in his family tend to die young. I know that he will leave you his own advice. As the firstborn girl, of a firstborn girl, of a firstborn girl, of a firstborn girl, of a firstborn girl, of a firstborn girl, I know you already have the strength that comes from that kind of matriarchal lineage. Here are some words of wisdom from your great-great-grandmother, your great-grandmother, your grandmother, and me.

GREAT-GREAT-GRANDMOTHER (GRAMMIE HALE)

Don't bite your nails. Nails go directly to the heart, and when you die and the doctors examine your heart, it will be all punctured with nails. [Good advice, bad reason.]

Always own a home with a hole in the center. Do no housework, just push everything down the hole, so you can spend your time doing creative things. [Good idea, but I was never able to find the hole.]

Don't tell anyone your "business." If you don't want it as tomorrow's headline, keep it to yourself. Don't tell "family tales." [No comment, for obvious reasons.]

Don't look at strangers, talk to them, or go with them. They will take you to a forest with a warren of underground tunnels—filled with kidnapped children—and do Bad Things [never elaborated] to you.

Be vigilant about your bowel movements. Check them for signs of bad color or content, and report them immediately. [She never said to whom.]

Never go on amusement-park rides. Your insides will get scrambled and they will never return to the right place. [What can I say?]

Don't put anything in your mouth that you picked up from the ground. Remember the boy who ate a piece of popcorn from the ground that an octopus had crawled into. And the octopus grew and grew inside his stomach until one day it exploded and the boy died. [Form your own conclusion.]

GREAT-GRANDMOTHER (GRANDMOTHER COONEY)

Don't ever get more education than your husband. It will ruin your marriage. [Disregard.]

There is nothing more important than family. [Have it tattooed on your hand.]

The beach is the best place for healing—hydrotherapy and heliotherapy can get anyone back on track. [I totally agree.]

Monitor your soul and your bowels closely. Saturday evening is a good time for a complete cleaning: confession, a bath, and an enema—whether you need it or not. [I will leave this for your own interpretation.]

GRANDMOTHER (GRANDMOTHER MANNING)

Boys are like streetcars—one comes along every few minutes. [Which, in the recounting from me to Sarah to Priscilla, became, "Boys are like streetcars. You get off one, you get on another." Feel free to chose either the Thomas Wolfe version or the Aunt Priscilla version.]

Always keep the kitchen clean. The rest of the house can go to hell, but if the kitchen is clean, you can cope. [True.]

On suffering: Offer it up for the souls in Purgatory. [Someone might as well get something out of it.]

No one can embarrass you but yourself. [Good advice—and the possibilities are endless.]

If you can't say something nice, don't say anything at all. [Nice sentiment, but then there is 50 percent less to say.]

Don't get weighed more than once a year. [Is that possible?]

Pay as little attention to your bowels as your health will allow. [Thank God.]

When people say, "How are you?" remember that they are not looking for a health report. [True.]

Life's not fair. Get used to it. [Correct, but try to find a gentler way to say it.]

Put ice on it. [Depends where.]

MY ADVICE

Always be suspicious of a person, a restaurant, or a hotel that describes itself with *clean* as the first adjective. If that is its best quality, I have serious reservations about the honesty or relevance of anything else on the list.

Economy is another terrible word. *Cheap* is better. Economy implies that you're getting a good deal. Cheap says it's inexpensive and makes absolutely no promises about quality.

Avoid anything that advertises itself as "family style." Family style is a euphemism for chaos and includes all kinds of behaviors that I hope you will never tolerate in your own family. The bad news is that the food is always overcooked to the point of tastelessness. The good news is that you can have as much as you want. Family-style places allow you to compare your family against other people's—children running around like wild animals letting out fork-dropping, glass-breaking, mind-curdling screams, and older couples staring vacantly past each other as they eat like robots and wonder if they are having a good time.

If you insist on continuing to be a vegetarian, take vitamins.

I'm with my mother on the bowel thing.

Read a lot. Anything you can get your hands on. Roll around in language.

Delight in words. Know the challenge of finding the exact, best, perfect word to define your experience.

Let music continue to be your constant companion. Don't let your tastes fossilize. Try the new stuff. Dance whenever you can. Rock on.

Martha Manning

Learn to cook. I'm sorry I never taught you. Hopefully you've picked up something from your father.

Continue the rituals of our family. Add to them. Light the candles every Sunday evening in Advent. Fill the living room with at least fifty candles on Christmas Eve. Light every one of them. Allow everybody to open one gift. Appreciate the light as it flickers across the faces of the people you love. Write out elaborate rhyming clues for Easter egg hunts. On July 4, continue with the only baking I ever taught you—our annual flag cake. If you feel especially energetic, make another one like we used to on July 14, and try to sing "La Marseillaise" the whole way through. Use real whipped cream, raspberries, and blueberries. On Thanksgiving morning, contribute to the feeding of someone else. When you leave your children for trips, give them something they can open every night or morning. A letter, a lollipop—some concrete thing that lets them know you are thinking of them.

Celebrate each transition fully—birthdays, graduations, anniversaries, accomplishments. Observe loss and the memory of that loss over time. Do it enough the same way each year to give you a sense of tradition, and throw in something new to add your own imprint. Rituals are the punctuation marks in our lives. Don't get sloppy with them. Sometimes they are the only anchor in a life that feels adrift.

Cherish your friends. This will be more important for you than for many people. Because you are an only child, you will have to work harder at preserving a sense of family than I did. Remember that you can have family in any loving, cohesive group, even when no one is related by blood.

Even though it requires effort, stay in touch with your aunts, uncles, and cousins. A family helps you to remember who you are and what you come from. You know well the problems our family has faced. But you also know the wonders. Remember that you can have a great family no matter how many of its members are wrestling demons. In a family, the whole is always greater than the sum of its parts. The synergistic energy created in a good family is nourishment for a lifetime.

Love like crazy. When you're ready, commit yourself to someone entirely. Expect rough patches, and then expect boring patches that make the rough ones look good. Remember that love in a relationship changes, the same way that a person's face changes over time. But with care, the essence can remain intact. I remember lines from a poem by William Carlos Williams about his marriage: "We have survived to keep the jeweled prize always at our fingertips. We will it so and so it is. Past all accident." I believe that it takes more than sheer will to make a relationship work, but those lines have reminded me on numerous occasions not to let love slip too far away.

If it's possible, have a child. I hope you find a partner with whom to share your life. But don't wait too long for the child. My most impulsive and best decision was to have you when I was young and stupid, studying like hell to be smart on no money and a lot of hope. When I became smart, and reason took over, I planned my life, inserting the idea of more children at point A and then point B. As you know, it didn't work out.

If you have a child, give yourself generously to her childhood. Not just an hour in the evening after work, or on weekends. Break the rules about who should do what. But don't sacrifice the child in the name of anything. Remember Uncle Darrell and Uncle Greg, who stayed home with Chelsea and Tori while their mothers continued with their careers. Remember Aunt Ann, who stayed home while Uncle Chip worked, and loved it so much that she was unhappy when she needed to return to work. Remember Dad, rearranging his schedule for every field hockey game, for school trips. Expect a man to share fully in the nourishment of a child. Demand it of yourself as well. If it means that your careers coast for a while, let them coast. If it means making do on less money, make do. Don't accept anyone's bullshit that "working mothers" are responsible for the breakup of the family. Everyone is responsible for the family. But also don't delude yourself about the needs of children. They need a lot. Sometimes, more than you think you have in you. I'm not just saying this for the benefit of your child. I'm saying that you should do it, also, for yourself. Being a mother is the best thing I've ever done with my life. But a number of years passed, when I was struggling with other things, before I realized that.

Find work that you love—even if it's not the work you're getting paid for. Make sure there's always a fire burning someplace in your life. It makes the rest of it bearable. Take chances. Screw up. Don't be polite. It's a total waste of time.

Ask for help when you need it. Know that it is a sign of character and not, as I used to think, a lack of it.

Find a spiritual home. I don't care what religion it is. But give yourself to some belief, to some sense of worship, for awe of that which is beyond you. Read the writings of the many holy women and men through the ages. Their words can infuse your life with direction and purpose. Pray. Work for justice and peace. Know your own strength. Don't let the gravity of the status quo paralyze you and make you complacent. Allow a place in your life for righteous anger.

Don't get too attached to stuff. Everything around you will tell you the opposite. But remember the first time I went to that ritzy shopping mall after those horrible years of depression, ending with the hospital and ECT. Remember how I said that I felt like a Martian and everything looked crazy to me? Well, it wasn't just because I was crazy. You and Dad blanched when I said I wanted to stand up on a chair and yell, "You people . . . go home . . . what you're looking for . . . I swear, it's not here!" But that was actually one of the sanest moments of my life. Take pleasure in the things you have. But always ask yourself whether the thing you're dying for at the moment is something you *want* or something you *need.* Wanting is okay; just don't let it masquerade as needing. It screws up your decisions. If you go offtrack on this, just drive slowly through the poorest part of the city, or take a working trip to a third-world country. Look for women your age. Look for children. Think again about the difference between your need and theirs, between your want and theirs.

Get comfortable with your body. Treat it well. Put it to work. Give it rest. Let yourself love the way you look. I can't give you any more advice on that. I never got that far.

Make friends with silence. Know the grace of your own company, and I promise, you will never be alone.

Acknowledgments

AS AN UNSCHOOLED WRITER I value the "on the job" education I have received from my editors over the past several years. There are times when the editing process feels like surgery without the anesthesia, but the vast majority of my experience with editors has actually approached the level of "fun." Unlike the dreaded red marks on the papers of my childhood, these newer ones invite me to consider alternative ways of thinking, talking, and painting pictures with words. My thanks to editors Michael Anderson, Katy Butler, Betsy Carter, Meg Cohen-Ragas, Frank Cunningham, Mary Lynn Hendrickson, Caroline Herron, Cindy Levy, Peggy Northrop, Meinrad Scherer-Emunds, Emma Segal, and Richard Simon.

Collaboration with my editor Barbara Moulton has been one of those marriages of minds that happen rarely. She is a wise companion on the uncertain journey that begins with a half-baked proposal and ends with a completed manuscript. With an elegant gentleness she points out paths and points I've never considered, and calls me away from those same tired places I favor when I am afraid.

Many people at Harper Collins San Francisco have contributed to the publication of this book. I thank especially Lisa Bach, Judy Beck, Lisa Zuniga Carlsen, Nancy Fish, Laura Galinson, Tom Grady, Laura Harger, Mary Peelen, Susan Reich, Robin

Seaman, Michele Wetherbee, and all of the sales representatives of Harper Collins for their care and enthusiasm.

I hit the jackpot when Arielle Eckstut of James Levine Communications became my agent. She takes better care of me than I take care of myself. I admire her tremendous command of literature, her talent, and her integrity. In short, I'm crazy about her.

I thank the nuns of my childhood—the good ones for being some of the best models of working women in the fifties and sixties, and the bad ones for the great material.

The Catholic Relief Services and Jack Morgan invited me to El Salvador and Honduras, which forever altered my perceptions of poverty and responsibility.

I am grateful to Patricia Dalton for the constancy of her friendship and her gift of Yeats.

I am grateful to the monks at the Holy Cross Abbey for allowing me access to their holy place, and to Tom and Nancy Ryan for initiating me into a love affair with the Maine coastline.

My large and lively family is rich with storytellers. I especially thank my mother, my father, and my aunt Nancy Ryan and my uncle David Cooney for entertaining me for hours and connecting me to my more distant past.

I also thank the brothers and sisters with whom I have shared times so vivid that I have to remind myself that we are no longer children, even though we still sometimes act like it. The trials of the past year have brought sweet recognition of the many blessings of membership in my family.

Due to an unfortunate pronoun incident, my sister Rachel was incorrectly labeled an alcoholic in the cloth version of *Undercurrents,* my previous book. She endured many awkward moments as a result—always with grace and good humor. For that I thank her.

My husband, Brian, and my daughter, Keara, are learning how to tolerate me when I write, reserving (for the most part) questions like "Isn't that the same flannel nightgown that you wore all day yesterday?" or "How long has it been since you looked in a mirror?" They leave me lost in thought when I need it and pull me back when it looks like I could get lost forever. Every single day I feel lucky to love them and even luckier that they love me. Through them I've learned that chasing grace is no longer necessary. Wherever they are, grace is.

Permissions